The Resurrection Network

Michael Manley

Kathy –
you have God's
blessings in all you do...
enjoy!
Mike

The age of the universe as measured via
Planck Collaboration, 2015…

13.799 +/- 0.021 billion years.

Hippocratic Oath…
With regard to healing the sick…I will take care that they suffer no hurt or damage.

Pope Francis: The fight against abortion is "part of the battle in favor of life from the moment of conception until a dignified, natural end. This includes the care of the mother during pregnancy, the existence of laws to protect the mother postpartum, and the need to ensure that children receive enough food, as well as providing healthcare throughout the whole length of life…" His Life in His Own Words. Published by Penguin Group (USA) LLC.

Siddhartha Gautama, the Buddha: One moment can change a day, one day can change a life, and one life can change the world.

Mohandas Gandhi: Where there is love, there is life.

Declaration of Independence: We hold these truths to be self-evident, that all men are created equal, that they are endowed by their Creator with certain unalienable Rights, that among these are Life, Liberty, and the pursuit of Happiness.

Nazi Germany statement on eugenics:
The Marital Health Law of October 1935 banned unions between the "hereditarily healthy" and persons deemed genetically unfit. Getting married and having children became a national duty for the "racially fit." In a speech on September 8, 1935, Hitler proclaimed, "In my state, the mother is the most important citizen." Jewish Virtual Library.

Theodore Roosevelt: The darker the night, the bolder the lion.

CHAPTER 1

There was no time to scream. She sensed, rather than felt, the rear wheels of her Toyota Corolla drift to the right on the rain-soaked highway. The sensation brought that confirming and immediate surge of panic-a simultaneous flash of awareness and dread that alerts the reflexes and blinds conscious thought. Her mind, recognizing deliberative thought as too cumbersome a process to survive the danger at hand, surrendered her nervous system to her only hope, intuitive reflexes and just plain dumb luck.

Neither prevented the rear of the small gray Toyota from mounting the guardrail and being launched, spinning clumsily into the rainy Pennsylvania night.

The driver, oblivious to the pathetic absurdity of her actions, was standing on the brake and jamming the steering wheel to the right in the airborne Toyota. The car slammed into the ground and flipped three times. She was unconscious before the car came to rest, upside down, its trunk intruding into the shallows of the Lackawaxan River that ran parallel to the roadway.

Her shoulder was pressed against the bloody driver's side window. The seat belt held her twisted and broken body in what little space remained between the steering wheel and the door. The engine protruded into the passenger's side of the front seat. It sputtered and died and the smell of gasoline filled the car.

Headlights from a car a quarter mile behind cut through the night air above the barely recognizable Toyota before its one remaining rear wheel stopped spinning. The child in her womb stirred.

****

At 6 a.m. the iPhone of Dr. Edward Tully rang as he was paying for a take-out order at a nearby coffee shop. He glanced at the number code. It signaled a coded message to call the hospital immediately – Emergency. He quickly gave the clerk $10.00 for the two chocolate glazed doughnuts in the bag. "Keep the change," he said as he reached for his phone as he hurried out the door.

Across town the vibrating hospital-supplied phone of Dr. Joan Evans alerted her to the emergency that was taking place. She sighed. She was starting to prepare an early breakfast with her husband, Alan, their six-year-old twins, Adam and Joseph, and four-year old daughter, Amy. It was a family tradition; everyone was up at dawn to the oompah-pah of a Sousa march. Smiles were encouraged as they marched to the breakfast table. Given her unpredictable hours as a doctor and her husband's unpredictable hours as an attorney, they had agreed to make time for their family first thing in the morning. Even so, her duties at the hospital sometimes intruded. She excused herself, went to the direct-line hospital phone in the den. Moments later she returned to the kitchen and announced she had to go to the hospital and asked her husband to help clean up the dishes. He instinctively frowned, "Today?"

"I know Al, I'm sorry…"

"Does Mommy have to go?" asked Amy.

"Mommy has to help a sick person, sweetie. It's another mommy and she needs my help. But I'll be back soon," she said as she forced a smile. The boys smiled, too, but for a different reason. They knew how to "play" their father for an extra "Little Debby" breakfast cake. "Sorry, Alan, hazards of being on-call," she said as she kissed her husband goodbye. "I'll call you later."

Within minutes Doctors Tully and Evans had joined the trauma team working on the pregnant woman the hospital rescue squad had helped free from the wreck several hours earlier. The trauma team employed a straightforward protocol for multiple surgical procedures. However in this small town, there was usually more preparation and practice than was the need. The written policy was to treat multiple injuries as if they occurred one at a time, but in order of importance to sustain life. In this case the head trauma would be addressed first with surgery to relieve any pressure on the brain. A second team would then work on the compound fracture of the left leg. A third team of obstetricians would be on standby to attempt to deliver the baby via C-section in the unforeseen event that the patient died on the table, or if she went into labor. The surgery, if limited to the head trauma and compound fracture, would take about six hours. It was 7:18 a.m. when the patient was wheeled into OR3.

An hour later, Noreen Ryan, R.N., the professional liaison to the hospital administrator, Doug Fedderson, walked into his office carrying two Grande containers of Starbucks coffee. She was awakened by an urgent phone call two hours earlier from the ER apprising her of the auto accident and hasty admission of the pregnant girl.

He looked at her. "Oh, oh! Two coffees? No pastries, what happened?"

It was part of her job to brief Fedderson on any unusual cases admitted to the hospital. She would prepare an outline of the medical considerations of the case and interpret all medical and legal issues that would affect both the hospital and the patient. Special attention was paid to any admission that might affect the bottom line of the hospital budget.

Doug Fedderson arrived at 8:15 every morning. On the job for 16 months, Fedderson was single and in his late 30's. He had left a challenging career at a prestigious Manhattan hospital to work at Lake Veterans Memorial Hospital in the woodsy lake region of the Poconos. The selection committee was impressed with his resume but doubted his sincerity in re-locating to this rural community. Mrs. Hubbard, the doyenne of the committee couldn't help but question his motives for the move from a challenging position with a big city hospital with its hefty salary, perks, and prestige to a, well, bona fide small town hospital with its commensurate small town salary in the off-beat town of Honesdale. She described his moves in an altered form of the Young and Lewis lyrics, "How ya gonna keep 'em down on the farm after he's seen Paree?"

They met with him several times before offering him the positon. They reasoned that if he kept driving to the meetings, it must be some indicator of his personal resolution to make a change. They appreciated his background with responsible positions in New Orleans and Houston prior to New York. And, he came highly recommended and interviewed very well. Nevertheless, after he accepted their offer, rumors of back room deals and large donations to the hospital from mysterious sources made the rounds. And there were others who said his certifiable bachelor-hunk status won over several women on the selection committee. These rumors, said his supporters, just demonstrated the rural community's wrongheaded conservative attitudes about women and testosterone; and an overriding dislike and distrust of anything or anyone from New York City.

For his part Fedderson ignored the rumors. The job was important to him and he saw no reason to apologize for any of the support he received. Since taking the job, Fedderson's cautious, careful, and thrifty management style had won over a number of former opponents who now seemed willing to ignore all the Big Apple, Big Easy, and Space City connections. In fact, thanks to several donations he easily seemed to secure, the overall debt had been reduced by 20% and plans were being made for a 50-bed addition to the hospital.

"The patient," reported Nurse Ryan, "is a 24-year-old pregnant woman whose car left the road and turned over into the creek about 16 miles west of the city. The driver of a passing car observed the accident and phoned 911. The time of the call was 3:31 a.m. Our mobile EMT team was on-site about 30 minutes after the one car accident." She glanced at Fedderson and added, "The 30 minute response time is

acceptable when factoring time of day and distance traveled."
She continued, "According to the EMT Report, they needed to
employ the 'jaws of life' to free the driver". Ryan was
referring to the hydraulically powered prying tool that has the
capability of ripping open a car door, roof, or any part
necessary to access the occupants and get them out safely. "As
of 15-minutes ago, Dr. Tully is unclear as to the degree or
extent of the head injuries. The patient remains unconscious,
her vital signs are improving, but there are some concerns
about the pregnancy. The accident was pretty violent according
to the initial on site State Police report."

    "Pregnant, you said?" He sipped the coffee and
walked to an office window. He glanced out at the mobile
EMT unit parked below his second floor office. "Which team
was on duty?"

    Ryan glanced at her notes. "Oh, let's see. Um'm.
Looks like McGuinness's crew."

    "Good. She got the best of the best," he smiled
recalling his first day at Lake Veterans. Luke McGuinness was
on EMT duty that day and one of the first persons to welcome
him to Honesdale. He offered him coffee and aspirin as he
signaled what kind of hospital team he was joining. Since that
time, he and Luke often traded "Hi-5s," "Gotcha's," and "How
was your weekend?" comments but nothing more than that.
Different pay scales, responsibilities, and social environment
he thought separated them. But in reviewing the monthly EMT
reports, he noticed McGuinness' team results was always
above par, his management skills were on the highest level and
his knowledge of hospital protocol outstanding. Something
about him was different from the rest of the hospital
management team, he reasoned. He waved to McGuinness as
he turned from the window. McGuinness noticed him and
waved back.

    "Noreen, what trimester? Who's her regular OB-
GYN?"

    "Mid to late third trimester is our initial best guess.

We're still testing. Will have stress results in due time. As for her regular OB-GYN or any other medical information, we only know what's on her driver's license: O-positive blood and not an organ donor."

"So it could be our birthing team," he offered. "Have they been alerted?"

"Dr. Evans has been alerted."

What else do we know about her?"

"Not much. She's from Starrucca, a short distance away. The police are checking out her residence, an apartment, and looking for next of kin, friends, lovers, or pets." When she referred to "pets", Ryan was following procedure to check whether she had a dog or cat. The police would search for any pet and look for pet collar information which might indicate the name of the local veterinarian who might have given the animal any routine treatment. Oftentimes in this rural community, the vet knows more about a family than the siblings. "People talk to the vet as if we were their confessor," Doc McGraw would often say. "I've heard more stories about stray relationships than stray pets, and some of those stories made me blush!"

"When can we get an update?" asked Fedderson as he sipped his hot coffee.

"It's touch and go. She'll be in surgery until 2 or 3 this afternoon. Dr. Tully wants to see you when he's done."

"Thanks, Noreen," Fedderson said excusing her. He glanced out the window and noticed Luke McGuinness conducting some sort of training with his crew. They again waved to each other. Fedderson walked to his desk. He took a newly purchased disposable cell phone from his top drawer desk. He dialed and waited. He left a message on a recorded line. He hung up and powered off the phone. He placed the phone back into the Wal-Mart bag and placed it in his briefcase.

A little before 3 p.m., Ryan notified Fedderson that Tully and Evans were out of surgery and ready to discuss the case with him. They met in his office. After pouring coffee and offering lunch to the Chiefs of Pediatrics and Obstetrics, Fedderson began.

"So, how is she?"

"Critical, but stable," said Dr. Tully.

"And the baby?"

"Well," said Dr. Evans, "the patient arrived partially dilated, two centimeters. But there's been no change since then. We hope she can hold off full labor for as long as possible. We don't know if she can survive the stress of another procedure. As for the fetus, there are no evident injuries. A team will be systematically monitoring the baby's stress level and the laboratory results and reporting later today."

Tully added, "The woman's head injuries were serious with massive blood pressure on the brain for an extended time. Triple C's," he added. "Contusions, concussion, and comatose," said Tully. "Judging from my observation there is most likely some form of brain damage. Cognitive impairment is most likely in cases like these, and it might be severe. There's no way to know if she'll come out of the coma, however. To tell you the truth, I'm surprised she got to the hospital alive. Credit the good work, no, the great work of McGuinness' EMT team."

"I understand the leg was a nasty bit of work, too," said Evans referring to the surgical team that re-set the multiply broken femur. "All in all, our girl has had a tough day. The next 36 hours are critical. We're prepared to deliver if she goes into labor. Obviously, we'd prefer she didn't just yet."

"Let's hope not. What do we know about the patient," said Fedderson nodding to Ryan.

"Thanks, Doug, the police have checked out the woman's apartment with no indication of any roommates or living relatives, or pets. No address book. Her neighbors say she wasn't married, and say they don't know who the father is. She works as a receptionist for a small real estate office. The local police contacted the real estate owner who said that she's been there for six months. She said she wasn't aware of her having a steady boyfriend. She believed her co-workers would describe her as "friendly". According to the realtor, she never even mentioned the father's name to anyone. For now, we don't know whether there are next of kin or even if the father of the child is in or out of the picture."

"Well, shouldn't we bring the hospital's attorney into this just to cover all the bases?" asked Dr. Evans.

"Joan, you are sounding more and more like a hospital administrator all the time. Are you sure you're not fishing for my job?" he said jokingly as he changed the tenor of the meeting.

"The only fishing I'm going to do is the May Day Family Fishing Derby over at Peterson's Pond. Last year my Amy was too young. But this year she's planning to have a coffee can full of night-crawlers by contest time and has already challenged her brothers for the biggest, ah, what kind of fish do we catch in that pond, anyway?"

"A fish is a fish is a fish," said Fedderson hunching his shoulders. "Now tell me, Joan, why do you think we need to involve the hospital attorney?"

She smiled thankful that she was asked her opinion. She liked the way Fedderson's focus on transparency and inclusiveness was changing the hospital's morale. "Well, we've got an unconscious patient, no family members to make decisions on her behalf, no one to let us know her wishes. We may be faced with medical choices that put the mother at risk in order to save the child or that could put the child at risk in order to save the mother." She drummed her pencil on the chair. "Suppose, for example, that we make the best choices we medically can and then two months down the road a long-lost aunt, or husband, or the father of the child comes out of the woodwork with plans to sue the pants off us all. In short we are flying blind without a medical directive."

"You do have the makings of a hospital administrator," said Fedderson with a broad smile.

"I see no reason to resort to personal insults here," said Dr. Evans, smiling her rejoinder. "I'm just expressing an opinion."

"I agree with Joan," said Dr. Tully.

"As do I," said Fedderson reaching for the phone and dialing the law firm of Davidson, Modell, and Shapp. "Let's get some bona fide legal advice." The phone rang.

"Good morning, Davidson, Modell, and Shapp. How may I direct your call," a pleasant sounding young woman answered. "Vivian Modell please, this is Doug Fedderson at Veterans Memorial, thanks." There was a pause. "Yes, Vivian, hello."

"Good afternoon, Doug," Vivian whispered in her most seductive voice. "What can I do for you today, or prepare for you for dinner tonight for that matter?"

Except for turning slightly red, Doug was thankful he hadn't put the call on speaker-phone. He couldn't understand why he, a grown man, would still blush when he talked with Vivian. After all, she wasn't his first romance and he was still unsure whether she would be his last. He was never truly confident about their relationship because she once termed it a "rebound" after her break-up with a town police detective. But he ignored the "dinner" comment from Vivian, whom he had been dating for the better part of a year. "I'm sitting in my office with Doctors Tully and Evans. We have a situation that requires your legal services."

"OK, it's business before pleasure. Can we cover this on the phone, or should I come by?"

"How quickly can you get here?"

"Sounds serious, I'll be right over, sweetheart," she couldn't help add as she smiled.

As he hung up the phone he again lectured himself about getting involved in an office romance. He knew better, but that didn't seem to matter when it came to Vivian. And besides, he argued, she wasn't really in the office, just the attorney representing the hospital. Hell, he thought, we're both adults. He was her client. No matter how innocently he tried to phrase it, the overlap between his professional and personal relationship with Vivian always retained an unpleasant tinge of scandal, of impropriety. Potential fodder for wagging tongues which was a cottage industry in Honesdale.

"Vivian Modell will be right over," he said, clearing his throat uncomfortably.

Doctors Tully and Evans exchanged glances. They knew why Fedderson became flustered as he was talking with Modell. The entire hospital, the whole town for that matter, knew about the "goings on", as Mrs. Hubbard called it. Nobody seemed to mind. The keepers of the standards who passed judgement on such arrangements had decided that Doug and Vivian made a nice couple. They felt that Vivian, their hometown girl, was more than a match for any slick hot shot New Yorker.

Dr. Evans, attempting to break the tension, said, "I think it's a credit to Vivian's professionalism that she responds to your needs, I mean, the needs of the hospital so quickly."

Ignoring the *faux pas*, Fedderson simply shook his head and responded, "She's an excellent attorney."

Modell's office was only minutes away. Vivian had joined a local law firm six years before, after graduating from law school. Although the firm handled the legal affairs of several large acreage local farmers and occasionally fostered land development and construction projects, its connections with "old Mainline Philadelphia money" was its primary source of work. The firm often thought of relocating to that city but its image was "honesty with a country climate". The partners decided to stay where it all began some 50 years earlier.

Vivian was remarkable in every respect. In her late 30's she exuded confidence, grace, and tenacity. She had options in life running the gamut of select schools (she chose Brown and Yale Law), to boyfriends and fiancées (there were two dusty rings on her nightstand-both men suggested she keep

16

the ring, and she did!), to specialty law practice (she relished the country life associated with living in the rustic lake community of northeastern Pennsylvania). Above all she was disciplined. Her daily regimen included an hour of yoga and exercise. At 5'10" (without heels) all eyes were on her when she walked into any room. It was said that her physical beauty and aura entered the area 5 minutes before she did.

She specialized in the social conscience side of the practice, which included a good bit of pro bono work. Her assignment to the lucrative hospital account seemed a natural extension of her charity work, and her outstanding performance had underscored the correctness of that decision. Vivian also directed the firm's corporate image and public relations activities. Most of these duties included participating in cultural and art activities and supporting various charities. Vivian's primary charity was focused the children's wing of the hospital. Her outstanding charm and engaging personality made her an attractive public representative of the firm and her poise, tact, and easy manner made her equally comfortable in front of judges or TV cameras. Within three years, she was made a partner in the firm. She was part of the hospital selection committee that hired Fedderson, a fact that contributed grist for the rumor mill and, for those town residents who mistrusted Fedderson and kept hopes high for a messy and embarrassing end to the affair.

Vivian Modell entered Fedderson's office, "Hello, all."

"Vivian, thanks for coming, Doug quickly responded hoping to keep the conversation professional and hospital-focused."

"So what's so important that the hospital administrator and two department chiefs need to confer with the hospital attorney?"

Doug succinctly summarized the morning's events while handing her the outline of Noreen Ryan's notes. She quickly read the document.

"As I understand it -- this woman, by the way, do we

17

have a name for her?"

"Franco, Janice Franco," said Fedderson.

"So," continued Modell, "Janice is apparently an emancipated woman, over 21..."

"She's 24," said Fedderson.

"...with no known family members to approve or disapprove medical procedures. And our main concern is our vulnerability to litigation brought in the future by persons as yet unknown."

"That's it," said Fedderson.

"What is the current hospital policy in these cases?"

"We immediately call our esteemed and capable attorney to guide us," answered Fedderson.

"This esteemed and capable attorney would like a little more information on accepted medical procedures. Do we need to get the ethics committee involved?"

"That may be premature. We'll have to have more information first. From what I can tell, we haven't been through this before at Memorial. But there are similar cases elsewhere involving pregnancies," said Fedderson. "I've started calling around, playing phone tag with some of the larger hospitals, so I don't have anything yet..."

"Well, you've made a start," said Vivian. "Now, what's the likelihood of having to make a decision concerning the baby?"

Fedderson's phone rang. He picked up the receiver, muttered something under his breath and handed the phone to Dr. Evans.

"It's for you. Janice Franco is in labor."

Chapter 2

The hospital's diagnostic laboratory was located in the basement next to the X-Ray Department down the hall from Central Supply and the nurses' lounge. The generous gift of an anonymous donor enabled the hospital to greatly expand the size and scope of the lab. It seemed rather strange to some that the expanded capability was much more than was needed for such a small town hospital, but when someone else is paying the bill, who can say "No" to the expenditure? The expanded lab meant the mechanical and carpentry shops had to be re-located to an out building behind the hospital. The hospital morgue was then relocated next to the lab near a loading dock for "family privacy and convenience" or so said the hospital committee that authorized the changes.

Two days after the comatose Janice Franco gave birth to a baby girl Dr. Evans sat in the physicians' booth in the laboratory. The semi-private enclosure was designed so that physicians can review and consult with the laboratory chief. Its light caramel colored wood- grained paneled walls focused the soft overhead lighting to the work station desktop and medical records monitor where Evans sat. She was troubled as she reviewed the data. Although she was knowledgeable in laboratory analysis, she wanted an expert to sift the numbers and charts. She was hoping her diagnostic hunch was wrong. Although she graduated from Penn State-Hershey Medical School and her residency in obstetrics included extensive hours in diagnostic studies her skills were limited in differential diagnosis. She hesitated briefly before requesting outside consultation on the case. She knew she needed specific medical expertise, but didn't like the source of that expertise – Dr. Frederick Nichols.

Evans did not relish getting involved with Nichols. She realized his medical skills were first rate and he came highly recommended to the hospital. And she found him to be an effective and very competent pediatrician. But he was also at the center of a group of doctors, nurses, and other hospital staff that openly and, in Dr. Evans's opinion, improperly, mixed religion, politics, and medicine. Evans found their brand of religious activism distasteful and obtuse. At times she privately labeled it "downright scary." Dr. Nichols would (and did) argue that one's faith in God could never be out of place. He maintained the Hippocratic Oath was divinely inspired and often cited the life of the gospel writer and physician, St. Luke, to amplify his point.

She knew that Nichols disapproved of her stand on women's issues as well. He openly opposed her decision to donate her consulting and medical services one Saturday a month at a local family planning clinic. It was a narrow line to thread. She believed in women's issues: she championed equal pay for equal work, the need for equal consideration in both educational opportunities and medical services. When her daughter Amy was born, she decorated the hospital bassinet with Title 9 leaflets claiming, "one day she would excel at sports at Brown" She believed in the absolute need for a woman to control her own body. "It's me, it's mine, we sing together!" she cried in a moment of self-actualization. And yet, there were many times when she thought about the child she called Eve who would have turned 10 this past March. In those times of self-doubt and quiet, she would tell Alan that she could "almost hear the voice of Eve calling to her."

He felt helpless to help her. Initially, his attempts to rationalize dream interpretation proved successful. He'd suggest the dream was 'a trip to her past' but nothing more. When that explanation proved unfulfilling, Alan would urge her to reconsider her involvement with the clinic. She refused, as he knew she would. He always acquiesced to her clinic role because he didn't want to go through the "it's my body" ersatz logic issue for the umpteenth time.

Joan Evans' introduction to the clinic's purpose came in a roundabout and unexpected way. As a college student, she was part of a group of girls who never missed a frat party or football victory party or any gathering that had the word "party" attached to it. In fact, one Saturday night in the middle of the "dullest February in the history of Penn State" she gathered her coterie of friends and threw a "party-party". That's when she met Kirk, second string football team quarterback and first team in good looks. As she recalls the night, she doesn't know if it was too much beer, her screaming hormones, or the date rape drug he dropped in her half-empty Yuengling bottle, but whatever the cause, her fault his fault, whatever, she missed her period that month.

Ashamed, embarrassed, afraid, she found her way to the "clinic" as the college crowd called the off-campus family planning center. Staffed by a ready and willing professional staff, it dispensed free condoms and other prophylactic paraphernalia on a demand basis which usually served the weekend party crowd. All that free advice and health admonitions actually disguised an abortion mill mentality that served the college co-eds needs. She convinced herself that her parents wouldn't understand and she didn't want to stress them out, or cause them any shame so it was there on a Holy Thursday morning, that she signed consent papers and aborted her baby. She reasoned that now she could truly celebrate Easter with the family.

Baby Franco's condition forced her to consult with Nichols. If the diagnostic results about Baby Franco's condition were correct, Nichols's medical expertise would be needed. Earlier in the day she had put her personal feelings aside and contacted Dr. Nichols, and now she was watching the pediatrician stride confidently toward her as she stood by Baby Franco's bassinet in the neonatal intensive care unit.

Born and raised in New Orleans, Nichols traced his

lineage to the early 19th century. It was said that seven generations ago, one of his ancestors warned Andrew Jackson that the British forces had crossed Bayou Bienvenu thus beginning the Battle of New Orleans. Nichols still strode with the confidence of a war hero. He could easily be the model of a bronze statue or stone cutting by Michelangelo. Ruggedly good looking in his mid-40's he never married. "Too busy saving lives," he'd retort in his "N'awlins" accent when anyone tried to fix him up on a blind date. Some thought he was gay especially when he occasionally dressed colorfully like a Mardi Gras float. "Just call it Bourbon Street-themed civic pride," he would again say deflecting any thought of dating. Others believed he was wounded in an accident and ashamed to reveal the injury to any potential bride. Whatever the true reason, he kept his own counsel.

"Dr. Nichols, so good of you to respond so quickly," said Dr. Evans in her most professional demeanor.

"Got here as soon as I could, darlin'," he said in his pleasant New Orleans drawl. "How's this little one doin'?" he added as he glanced into the bassinet.

Evans bristled at Nichols's creole and bayou good old boy act but resisted the urge to insist she be addressed as "Doctor", or "Joan" rather than "darlin'". She believed that Nichols did this deliberately to bait her into an argument with him on women's rights and ultimately, abortion. But today was not the day to confront Dr. Nichols, she thought to herself. She wanted medical information from him, and would have to deal with the man, not the bigot she reasoned, to get it. She steeled herself and directed the conversation to the patient's condition, "Doctor, I have some real concerns about this baby girl."

"Yes, I heard about the accident and the C-section. Good job, sweetheart," he said, again with a most admiring inflection. He placed his hand in his lab coat pocket and fingered a wooden crucifix.

"Thank you, Doctor," said Evans. She was becoming irritated that her colleague had not yet picked up on her strict formality as an obvious indication of how she preferred to be addressed. Again, she suspected that he deliberately adopted the folksy and sexist façade to irritate her. "Two can play that game," she thought to herself. This steadied her resolve to remain professional. "You're not getting my goat today, you bastard," she thought while saying aloud, "We have a serious matter to deal with. The infant patient appeared normal at delivery, but yesterday she seemed listless and had no appetite. After numerous attempts we were able to get something into her, but then she began vomiting. Since then, there have been a series of convulsions and sudden spastic movements."

"Have we checked for blockage of the lower intestine?"

"Yes. There is no obstruction. However, liver and spleen appear enlarged."

"I see," said Nichols, "and subsequent feedings?"

"Same results. We may have to feed her intravenously, but before we do, I wanted your opinion. The lab results…"

"…Any indication of internal injuries from the accident?"

"Absolutely none, Doctor. Quite remarkable, really, considering the extent of damage to the car."

"Credit God's design, there is no safer place in the world than the womb. Usually, that is," he added as he glanced at Evans. He paused as he fingered the crucifix. "We'll, I'd better get started," he said as he gently turned the baby on her right side, listened to her heart and then flexed her left arm and left leg. "Dilation and tactile capacities appear minimal. Negligible motor activity, less than full tone, and overall lack of movement, h'm'm. Negligible reaction to stimuli. Her lack of alertness could be due to the stress of the accident and delivery, but I think not."

The examination took less than 20 minutes. When done, he stepped back from the hospital bassinet and just stared at the unnamed infant. When he spoke again the good old boy banter was gone. He studied the lab reports and slowly read the suggested diagnostic conclusion, "…Inclusion-cell (I-cell) disease, mucolipidosis II, [ML II]." He frowned and reflected. He knew the outcome of this autosomal recessive disorder. His mind raced through the medical dictionary to its symptoms highlighted by a failure to thrive, abnormal skeletal development, restricted joint movement, internal liver and spleen damage and most likely early death. His heartache recalled a similarly diagnosed baby several years ago who eventually died before her first birthday.

"Joan, how is the mother?" he asked in all sincerity.

"In the ICU, comatose. The head injuries are possibly life threatening. The delivery and other accident injuries have weakened her considerably. Even if she survives, we don't know if she'll ever regain consciousness. She appears to be as close to death as possible without an actual death certificate."

"Such a shame," said Dr. Nichols. "I think we share the same suspicions about our little angel here. We've got to check her protein levels. I'll make the call to increase iron and B12 supplements intravenously. Then we'll take a blood sample, wait two hours and take another. But I may need your help."

"He asked for help," she thought. "How so?"

"I have a church engagement that I can't break this afternoon. Would you be able to follow through at the lab? Make sure these samples get the highest priority. The lab results will tell us how she is progressing."

"Yes, of course. Now, Dr. Nichols, I'd like to ask a favor of you on behalf of our patient."

"Shoot."

"Would you consider taking this case? It looks like a

freebie; Ms. Franco's health insurance status is questionable. She may have fallen through the cracks."

"So much for the latest national health care plan regulations," he chided.

He looked at the child and sighed, and said, "I'll be glad to do it. Now, little one," he said, addressing the infant while reaching into his lab coat pocket, "here's a little something for you." He retrieved a small, delicate gold pin, a winged cherub, from the pocket and pinned it to the fabric on the inside of the bassinet and softly whispered, "Your own guardian angel to watch over you." He then turned to Dr. Evans to say, "I give these to all my patients. Reminds the parents, and me, that medicine can do only so much. My guess is this little one will need a strong guardian angel."

Evans was more annoyed than touched by what she continued to view as Nichols's penchant for blurring the line between religion and medicine. Nonetheless she managed a polite, "Very nice gesture, Doctor. A comfort for many, I'm sure."

Nichols gestured towards the baby, looked at Evans and decided this was the time to bring up the subject. "I know Dr. Evans that you disagree with my religious views. But I don't understand how you, a doctor dedicated to healing, someone who cares so deeply about children as you do, for infants such as this little one, how you can allow yourself to participate in abortions...."

"That is none of your concern," she snapped. She struggled to control her anger but could not disguise the sharp edge to her response. She realized her guilt was not assuaged, if it ever will. "Look, Dr. Nichols, my beliefs and my conscience are my own affair. As are yours; and as long as your beliefs don't get in the way of good medicine, I won't comment on them. Please afford me the same courtesy."

"But your beliefs do get in the way of good medicine," challenged Nichols. "Doctors killing healthy babies..."

25

Dr. Evans cut him off, "Damn it, Nichols, spare me your sermons. I am comfortable in my own faith and with my own conscience," she lied. "If you don't want to take care of this patient, I'll get someone else. If you do, let's limit our discussions to her care. There are some who would consider your views callous and gender-angst loaded. Why did you ever not marry?"

He didn't want to get caught in a non-sequitur discussion, nor did he want to win an argument and lose the war. Realizing this discussion could escalate to an argument and possibly a hospital ethics panel review, Nichols shook his head sadly. "You'll make arrangements with the lab, then?"

"Yes, I'll have them text the results to you. Call me when you've had a chance to analyze the results. Now, unless there are other medical issues we need to discuss about this case, I must go. I thank you for your professional help in this matter. Good day, Doctor."

"Good day, Doctor Evans. God bless you."

Dr. Evans's eyes flashed angrily at Nichols. Refusing to respond, she hurriedly stalked out of the neo-natal intensive care unit.

****

Nichols arrived at the hospital early the following day and went straight to the Diagnostic Laboratory. He was anxious to review the additional overnight testing results. They were basically the same as the initial results, as he feared. Nichols decided a brief prayer would steady his decision. He knew it could end in only one way. Remaining in his chair, he pushed himself away from the cluttered desk in the laboratory cubicle. He sat erect, laid his open hands on his lap with his palms upward. He placed his feet flat on the floor, closed his eyes and took several deep breaths to relax himself. He prayed silently for several minutes before dialing

Dr. Evans's office.

"Dr. Evans, this is Dr. Nichols. I'm afraid I've got bad news about the Franco baby. The lab results remain the same and confirm we do have a mucolipidosis, Inclusion-cell baby girl."

"What's the prognosis officially?"

"If she is a textbook case, and, really, there isn't much more that we could ask for, death is most likely 7 years at the very outside, usually much sooner but only after years of probable multiple infections, respiratory disease, abnormal growth. Could be quite painful and debilitating," said Nichols. "It's a waiting game for now. Massive vitamin therapy is part of the regimen." He paused letting his words sink in. He added, "Anything new on the mother?"

"No improvement. God, I hate these cases," said Dr. Evans.

"They are difficult for us all," said Nichols, "but we can't lose hope."

"Hope," scoffed Evans. "We've got a mother who may be in a permanent vegetative state, an infant with a fatal disease whose most optimistic prognosis is years of pain, stunted growth, and brain damage, and Lord knows, what else. Then perhaps, she dies of starvation or other multiple possibilities at the ripe old age of seven. A quick death is her best hope," she reacted.

"That is out of our hands," said Nichols.

"Perhaps not, Doctor. If the mother doesn't regain consciousness, and no relative comes forward, we may have to make a decision on whether to adversely modify treatment for the infant."

"I'll fight any attempt to discontinue treatment. Life for this child may be hard, it may be painful, but it is life and life is the only moral option. We will combine prayer with advances in medicine to decide her future."

"On that, Doctor, we disagree. There are other matters, the expenditure of extensive medical resources on a hopeless case, the quality of life, thwarting death rather than sustaining life. Medicine is science, Dr. Nichols. Focus on what's best for your patients rather than using religious arguments to make what should be medical decisions."

"But Joan, who speaks for the infant? Who are we to pass judgment on the quality of another's life? You are correct, though. There are other concerns, other issues at work here. I'm aware of the political and financial issues. But, I'm concerned not only for the patient, but also for the soul of medicine itself."

"The soul of medicine! Aren't you being overly dramatic, Dr. Nichols?"

"Dramatic! I ask you, Dr. Evans, when does wisdom enter the discussion? Choosing death over life, what does that do to us as doctors? We can choose to let her die, and reduce her exposure to pain and suffering. But when we do so we diminish our own humanity and re-define our capacity for compassion. Are we ending someone's suffering, or reducing our own exposure to suffering? Why does our yearning for a happy ending mean death for another? When our response to pain is to end life, we may say we have the patient's interests at heart. But how often does our profession facilitate death as a way to satisfy our need to control medical situations or satisfy our guilt? Guilt is for the confessional, pain is for medicine. We don't like the rules of the game, so we quit, and take the ball--medical treatment-- home with us. In these instances the patient's death makes our own lives more comfortable. When we embrace death over life we lose something precious."

"Forgive me, Doctor, but you sound like some glossy pamphlet on the issue. You talk in judgmental platitudes and absolutes. We're talking about human beings and terrible suffering. Anything I would gain from such suffering is something I can do without. It may be a shock, but some of us believe that there is no point in permitting an infant to suffer excruciating pain for years. She will be severely brain damaged, perhaps most likely lessened self-awareness or awareness of others. But you say none of that matters. You know what God wants us to do. I may not know what he wants, but my God does not insist that we use our medical knowledge to force this child to suffer needlessly."

"You cannot know the mind of God."

"But you can, right? Neither of us knows the mind of God, so we are left to make these decisions using facts, Doctor. Scientific facts. Medical facts."

"Facts, Dr. Evans, are only the starting point. What of justice, of ethics?"

"You don't use *medical ethics* in your arguments, you rely on religious and moral arguments," she strongly retorted.

"That's no weakness. I get suspicious whenever the word ethics is preceded by a modifier--medical ethics, journalistic ethics, political ethics, and business ethics. Ethics alone should do. Right is right in every situation, no exception. But every profession conveniently carves away its ethics from the bedrock of genuine morality to justify unethical behavior. That is how abortion is justified," said Dr. Nichols.

Feeling exhausted, she capitulated. "Please, Doctor, let's not argue. Abortion has nothing to do with this case. This is the last time I will make this point with you. Confine yourself to medical facts on this case or I will have you removed and assign another physician. I can easily cite science and medical ethics as the reason. Is that clear?"

"Quite clear," he said realizing he had made his point and again, not wanting to win the battle and lose the war. "Now, if you will excuse me, I have patients to attend to. Goodbye," said Nichols, hanging up the phone.

In her office, Dr. Evans slammed the handset of her phone onto the cradle. She got up and walked to her office window, and looked out onto the well-landscaped grounds. It was a typical overcast March day. Spring wasn't yet in the air, but there was rain and the suggestion of green where the sun, when it was able to appear at all this time of year, lingered longest on the lawn. "Damn him," she whispered.

Fedderson was finishing a phone call. He hung up and placed the TracFone in his briefcase. "One more call on this baby and I'll burn it," he mumbled to himself. He left his office and walked down the hall. He met Vivian along the way. "Perfect timing," she said. They walked together towards the elevator. "You seem distracted," she added. She briefly kissed him on the lips. He smiled. "I was."

"I've several ideas I'd like to discuss with you and Dr. Evans."

"That's where I'm headed."

"We'll travel together. Two on a journey is better than one," she smiled. "I might have some answers for you on your impending dilemma."

"Answers I can use and please don't use the word 'dilemma'. It sounds confused and, after all, I'm a professional hospital administer – and I have all the answers." They took the elevator to the second floor and exited. They turned right. They stopped at Room 222 and knocked at the door.

"It's open," Evans said, without turning away from the window.

"Hello, Dr. Evans. Aren't we looking pensive," said Fedderson, upon entering the room.

"Hi Doug, Vivian," she nodded. "Doug, I just got some bad news about Baby Franco," said Dr. Evans, turning to face the hospital administrator.

"As you feared..."

"Yes. Nichols says it's just a matter of time -- days, months, maybe a few years.

"Damn."

"By the way, the good doctor and I had a fairly intense discussion on the baby's future. He may complain."

"Oh? What about?"

"Can't you guess?"

"I suppose I could, but why don't you tell me, for the record, in front of the hospital attorney. No, on second thought make your remarks off the record in front of our hospital attorney," he smiled at Vivian.

"It's his conservative, right-to-life attitude. He never misses an opportunity to attack me for my work at the clinic, and when I suggested that we may eventually have to consider modifying treatment for the infant he started one of his sermons. I should have known better than to bring up the subject. It's not an argument you can win with him."

"Nor an argument he can win with you."

"I suppose not. But one of us is wrong."

"Forget who's right or wrong," he said not wanting to enter that debate. "Let's hope we won't have to decide whether treatment should be amended. Vivian has some ideas on that score."

"Like what?" she said looking at Modell.

"So long as I don't get dragged into your disagreement with Dr. Nichols," she rolled her eyes. "My suggestions cover two basic options, although either might lead to the same place. One, have the child named as a ward of the state. Essentially the state adopts the child and appoints an attorney as guardian to represent the interests of the patient. The guardian has the authority to petition the court concerning treatment options."

"And the hospital's position?"

"Neutral, of course. We would provide medical testimony, but we wouldn't take one side or the other."

"Can you see Dr. Nichols providing neutral testimony?"

"No, and that is why I prefer the second option."

"Which is?"

"To use our friends in the press."

"The press!"

31

"Sure, newspapers, radio, TV, they'd be all over this. I can see the headline: <u>Comatose Mystery Mom, a Fatally Ill Baby, Unknown Father, No Known Family</u>, she said waving her hands in the air. "Network coverage is a sure thing. This could be a national story. *The Times*, Fox News, add Face Book, Twitter, whatever."

Fedderson smiled. "Sounds interesting."

She added, "Besides, there is no guarantee the press won't jump on this if we go straight to court. The publicity just might bring the father or some other relatives forward. We then have the family member go to court to be named the legal guardian of the mother and child, and voila, we are out of the life and death decision loop."

"You mean out of the liability loop, that's the important thing," Doug added.

"Yes, that is just a very happy side effect of having a family member make this decision. I can't deny that it's my job as legal counsel to look out for the welfare of this hospital. For us to make decisions now and face family members later could lead to years of litigation and cost hundreds of thousands of dollars. We've got better uses for that money than to purchase summer homes for lawyers."

"My, my. Harsh words about the legal profession coming from someone I'd have thought would harbor a more conciliatory view," Fedderson interjected.

"I was speaking of the billing policies of our potential legal adversaries only," Vivian smiled in return.

"Naturally. By the way Vivian, did you consider that once you invite the press to this party they may overstay their welcome?"

"Meaning?"

"If no relative comes forward the press will still be interested in the case. Our every move will be under the microscope. Do we want that?" he suggested.

"H'm'm!" Vivian responded.

"And really, the chances of the father coming

forward are slim. This is no knight in shining armor. He faded deep into the background when his responsibilities involved a healthy mother and child. What's going to make him step up now and take on heavier burdens?" Evans assumed.

Fedderson paused then thoughtfully added, "Frankly, I was feeling a lot better before I came in here."

"I'm sorry, Doug. I've upset you needlessly. Don't listen to me. I'm being overly pessimistic. Vivian is right: press coverage offers our best chance of having some family member come forward. And they are the ones who should be making these decisions."

He smiled, "First you scare the hell out of me, and then you try to reassure me. This approach does carry some risks, but it seems the best option at this point. Did I ever tell you the single most important perk this job offers?"

"No, what is it?"

"Readily available free aspirin. Every day is a new headache. See you later, Joan and Vivian. I've got to arrange a meeting."

****

After Doug Fedderson took two free aspirin he contacted members of the hospital's Board of Trustees and called an executive meeting for that evening. He briefly explained the need for the emergency meeting and outlined Vivian's two options.

He then phoned Vivian to confirm she would be able to attend the meeting.

"Maybe we'll have some time afterwards to discuss other matters," she baited him. He smiled on the other end of the phone and, taking the bait, said, "Yes, there are other issues we should be exploring."

In preparation for the Board of Trustees' meeting, Fedderson called for a written status report from each of the

physicians treating Janice Franco and her daughter. He
wanted the Board to be fully knowledgeable of the medical
issues at hand including Vivian's proposal for news
coverage. He realized this gathering of the hospital's most
influential physicians would tend to stake out boundaries of
medical jurisdiction right from the beginning so he asked the
Drs. Tully, Evans, and Nichols to be patient specific. He
requested they be present at the meeting and read their
reports.

Joan Evans reported that there did not seem to be any
complications relating to the cesarean section and that her
role as obstetrician was virtually over.

Dr. Tully gave a brief but disturbing report on Janice
Franco's condition and added, "Given the nature of her
injuries and the extent of intracranial pressure, it does not
surprise me that the patient remains comatose. We have
taken steps to reduce the pressure on the brain. There has
been some improvement. At this point, it is problematic
whether or not she will regain consciousness. Until she does,
the full extent of the insult to the brain cannot be assessed. I
am sorry to be so vague, but that's the best I can do at this
time."

"We're just looking for the best information
available, Doctor," said Fedderson, shifting his glance from
Tully to Nichols. "Well, Fred?" he prompted. "What have
you got for us?"

"Nothing pleasant, I'm afraid. All information posits
that this baby has an Inclusion Cell metabolic disorder.
Medically, we all know what that means," began Dr.
Nichols. "That makes this a disturbing and emotionally
wrenching case. I know that some in this room would argue
against continuing heroic medical efforts to sustain this
infant's life. Some here would argue against even routine
life-sustaining treatment, for what they see as a hopeless
case. I do not agree with that approach."

"Do you have an alternative?" asked Fedderson.

34

"Hope is always the alternative to despair."

"In medical terms," asked Dr. Evans, "what prospects do we have for hope?"

"In medical terms, perhaps, there are few reasonable prospects for hope. But in human terms..."

"Dr. Nichols, we have had this discussion before. Please limit your arguments to medical facts."

"Doug," said Nichols, turning to Fedderson for help, "as the attending physician for this patient I would like to be heard. I recognize the authority of the board and the hospital administration regarding continuation of treatment for this patient. I can assure you I will not publicly criticize whatever decision you make...if you let me make the case for continued treatment in this forum."

"Fair enough, Doctor," said Fedderson. "The floor is yours."

"Thanks, Doug. I won't take long. My point is simple: To continue treatment, no matter how hopeless that treatment may seem in conventional terms, offers the potential of at least one reason for hope--a medical miracle. The adage: 'Time heals all wounds' applies here. In medical research, time cures all. Why, it was only yesterday that penicillin was discovered and cured millions, this morning we found that a heart could be transplanted to save another's life, and maybe tomorrow we'll find a cure for this metabolic anomaly."

At this, Evans angrily rearranged herself in her chair and folded her arms across her chest while looking away from Nichols in disgust and shaking her head. The other occupants of the room also fidgeted in their chairs, bracing themselves for a lecture, as Nichols continued.

"Why so skeptical? We've all experienced medical miracles--sudden remissions, unexpected recoveries, and inexplicable healings. We know they happen. To withdraw or withhold treatment from this child of God would deny her, and us, any opportunity for a medical miracle.

"I know many of you don't agree with me. The board may not agree with me, the hospital administration may not agree with me." He looked around the room. He realized the tone of tension had driven the meeting to where he wanted it to be. He changed the character of his monologue. "Having said what needed to be said, and done what needed to be done, I am now prepared to deal with the probable decisions that will be made in the coming weeks concerning continuation of treatment for this patient." He paused for effect. "I have only one other remark to make and that is I want to go on record as taking personal responsibility for making and paying for funeral arrangements for this child, if such arrangements should be necessary while this patient is under my care." He paused again. "This is something I have done in the past for indigent patients and I would want to do so in this case. That is all I have to say on this matter."

Fedderson waited as the tension in the room diminished. But then he felt his own anxiety level increasing. "It was happening again. Change was coming again. The process is starting. Not now! And what about Vivian? Life was starting to get so comfortable with her," he thought to himself. "I wasn't absolutely certain that Nichols was the one. But I should have known it was him," he mentally chastised himself. "Now I've got to be careful, I mustn't make a mistake" he told himself as he gazed around the room. It was as if the hot air in a huge balloon was gradually letting out and the pressure crawled to zero. Everyone, including Evans took a deep breath.

Fedderson responded to the more relaxed tone. "Thank you, Doctor. I appreciate the sincerity of your comments and hope there will be no need to act on your very generous and compassionate offer." He decided a non-committal remark was the best reply he could make.

"Personally, Doug, I find prayer to be the most efficacious form of hope," added Nichols.

"I'm sure you do, Doctor. Now, if there are no further

comments...good, I would like to thank you all for your input. This is a difficult issue for the hospital but not as difficult, ultimately, as it is for this young woman and her daughter. This hospital administration and the board will endeavor to do whatever is in the best interest of these patients and this institution. Now, any other matters to discuss today? No. Well that about does it. That about covers everything for today."

As the meeting quickly broke up, Vivian remained seated across from Fedderson. "Doug, I have those papers for you to sign, if you have a moment," she said in voice loud enough to connote that he had other business to attend to and all others ought to leave the room. It worked. Doug closed the door and returned to where Vivian was sitting.

"I noticed you were taking quite a few notes during the meeting, Counselor. Is there anything pressing?" This time it was his turn to bait her.

"The only thing I want pressing is my body against yours, without the interference of these bulky clothes," she smiled in return.

He smiled in return and wondered how much time he had before it all fell apart. He hoped he could hold the relationship together but, in all reality, knew it was doomed. He, however, decided to enjoy the moment and would rationalize the guilt at a later time.

CHAPTER 3

Vivian Modell was right. The Janice Franco story generated a lot of interest. Several days later, the morning of the scheduled press conference Doug Fedderson met in his office with Vivian, Dr. Tully, Dr. Evans, and Dr. Nichols. Seated at a round table in Fedderson's spacious and tastefully decorated office, the five had gathered to again discuss their strategy and to ease their nervousness before facing the cameras and microphones of the ladies and gentlemen of the press. The coffee cups were near empty but the plate of donuts remained untouched.

The response to the announcement of the press conference had been greater than anyone at the table had expected. Due to the response, the midmorning press conference had to be moved from the main conference room and now took over about half of the cafeteria.

"Christ, Doug," said Tully, "What have we done? Did you see those vans in the parking lot? The lot is filled with vehicles sprouting satellite dishes and the ground is littered with cables going in every direction."

"It is a bit overwhelming, I know," said Doug. "But they'll be here only for another hour or two."

"Do we know who is represented?" asked Dr. Evans.

"On the TV side," said Vivian. "We've got the Scranton and Philadelphia affiliates of CBS, NBC, and ABC. The local Fox station has sent a crew. We've even got a couple of freelance video crews. They'll sell the footage to anyone they can, starting with CNN."

"If Dr. Evans and Vivian remove their blouses, it'll go to 'Entertainment Tonight'," said Dr. Tully wanting to reduce the tension.

"And if you disrobe, 'America's Biggest Loser' will get the call," was Dr. Evans's immediate response.

Their nervousness made each of the five laugh harder than the joke merited. The laughter felt good.

"What about newspapers?" asked Dr. Nichols.

"I don't know if the *New York Times* is here or not," said Fedderson, "but the *Scranton Times* sent their bureau chief and the *Philadelphia Inquirer* has a reporter and photographer here, so does the Associated Press. And then we have all the usual suspects, the local radio stations, and the free weekly neighborhood newspapers. All in all we've got quite a turnout. This is good."

"Doesn't feel very good," said Dr. Evans.

"C'mon, now," said Fedderson. "As doctors you face tougher situations every day. A few questions a few cameras. And don't forget the purpose of all this. The publicity may reach a family member. That would be best for the patients and the hospital. The most useless advice in the world is to tell someone not to be nervous, but if you are, don't act nervous. Certainly don't feel more nervous than I do."

"And how nervous is that?"

"Well, Vivian, when I have to speak to a crowd I sound like I'm speaking through a fan. I speak very quickly and my voice gets this vibrato quality, like my larynx is quivering in fear."

The others laughed.

"Before we go any further," said Nichols, "I want you to know that I won't be participating in this press conference."

"Fred, you're the attending physician of the child. It'll look odd. Why pull out now?" asked Fedderson as the others in the room turned to stare at Nichols.

"No secret, really. You all know how I feel. My beliefs conflict with some of the hospital's potential alternatives in this case. I've given my word to not disagree publicly with the hospital's policy. However, there are a number of questions that might be asked of me that, if answered honestly, would contradict hospital policy."

"So say 'No Comment'," suggested Dr. Evans.

"Not a good idea," said Vivian. "We've got to have a united front out there. Besides, if any of us says No Comment', that topic will then become the focus of the questioning. Far better to say I don't know or refer the question to Doug or to me."

"It seems," said Dr. Nichols, "we could avoid a lot of problems if I sit this one out."

"I'd prefer to have you on the dais with us, Doctor, but if this is how you want it, I respect your decision. Would you mind, though, staying in the room in case a question comes up that you should handle, rather than one of us?"

"That would be fine. I'll walk in with you and stand off to the side," said Nichols. He looked around the table, "Unless someone has some objections."

"OK by me," said Tully.

"Me, too," said Vivian.

"What do you say, Dr. Evans?" asked Nichols.

"Well, we can't force you to cooperate…"

"OK, OK, let's not give in to the tension here and start attacking…"

"You're right, Doug. I'm sorry Dr. Nichols. That was uncalled for."

"I forgive you, Joan. We're all under a lot of pressure," said Dr. Nichols.

Dr. Evans glared at Dr. Nichols. She could feel her anger well within her in response to Nichols's use of the word "forgive". Who the hell was he to forgive her? A simple "apology accepted" would have been sufficient, but not for Dr. Arrogance. He had to *forgive* her. He was always trying to stake out the moral high ground just so he could look down on others. Hypocrite! He reminded her of Fr. Gavigan, the chaplain at Penn State. After she confessed to him that she had an abortion, his counseling skills were more condemning than soothing. She can still hear his judgmental voice, "That's unconscionable, that's murder…why girl, why? But, I forgive you." Who was he to forgive? Wasn't God the one who

40

forgives? And the penance…to picket the clinic where I had the abortion! Had he never heard of a woman's right to her body?

Fedderson, sensing Dr. Evans's anger, quickly changed the subject before she could respond. "OK, now for the nuts and bolts of how this will go. We go downstairs as a group to the temporary stage in the cafeteria, go on stage, yadda yadda yadda, I'll welcome everyone, read the prepared statement…"

"Don't forget to introduce everyone," said Vivian.

"Right, right," said Fedderson. "I'll introduce each of you. By the way, everyone, please wear your nametags. It makes things much easier for the reporters."

"Why don't we write the article we want them to print and distribute it to them?" said Dr. Tully.

"We have" said Fedderson. "Everyone does. What did you think the press release and all the information in the press kit were for? You'd be surprised how often press releases are used virtually verbatim."

"The fact is," said Fedderson, "the easier we make it on the reporters, the less likely they'll become confrontational. But if we go too far, then they'll get insulted that we think we can lead them around like sheep."

"Which is what you want to do," said Dr. Tully.

"All I want," said Fedderson, "is an open, honest, spontaneous, and completely 'in-control-of-the-press' conference. Again, did I say 'in control'?" He smiled. " OK, so I welcome the press, introduce everyone on stage, read the prepared statement, make reference to the copies of Ms. Franco's driver's license photo in the press kits and then I'll open it up to questions. If a reporter does not address a question to one of us, I'll take it and if I can't handle it, I'll pass off to one of you.

"Any questions? OK, then. One last thing. We've been dealing with this issue for several weeks now. Indeed, we see tragedy and difficult human situations every day. We sometimes use humor to alleviate our stress. But what we say downstairs, how we act, will be seen and heard by people who don't know us and who might misinterpret a stress-relieving comment as a cavalier attitude, so, please, no attempts at humor."

"So I will be keeping my shirt on then," said Dr. Tully.

"Always the humanitarian," said Vivian.

"One that will be greatly appreciated by your co-workers," offered Dr. Evans.

"OK gang, time to throw ourselves to the lions," said Fedderson.

The five hospital representatives were silent as they walked to the elevator at the end of the hall. Fedderson pushed the down button and the elevator doors opened.

"A good omen, guys, elevator was at our floor, no waiting," said Fedderson cheerfully. Once the elevator doors closed the group again fell silent.

****

"So, honey," said Alan Evans, turning off the TV with the remote while giving his wife, Dr. Joan Evans, a kiss on the cheek, "what's it like seeing yourself on the 10 o'clock local news?"

"It's strange. Weird. There's a real sense of displacement. Like it isn't really me. Did you have to record it?"

"Your moment of fame? Of course. And you were great. And compassionate. You really got the point across about that poor child's suffering. Really, you were great."

"I thought Vivian came across well."

"Yeah, well she's been through that stuff before. It's old hat to her. She is obviously very comfortable in front of the camera," said Alan in an off-handed way as he turned off the digital video recorder.

"So, what are you saying, I didn't look comfortable?"

"Here it comes," he said mockingly, "the star

temperament. My friends warned me not to marry a beautiful media diva. 'She'll demand all your attention every minute of the day', they said. Did I listen? No, blinded by beauty, I fell…"

"Me demanding! Like you don't want all of my attention."

"I was certainly hoping for a little attention tonight."

"And you've never even been on TV," she said playfully, dismissing her husband with a wave of her hand.

"Not true. Well, technically true. But do home movies count? I mean I've been in dozens of them…some singing, some dancing, others more dramatic like crying when I toppled my ice cream cone onto the floor. Such great drama."

"What? We've been married eight years, known each other for ten, and I'm still finding out things about you."

"A man of mystery and very sexy, don't you think? Intrigue, romance, danger. What do you say…?"

"We're both practically movie stars."

"So much in common. It's fate. Made for each other. Or don't you date anyone in the business?"

"I may make an exception for you, once in a while anyway," she said laughing as he began to kiss her forehead playfully.

"Hey," he said. "Where was the bible thumper?"

"Nichols? He was there, but he refused to be on stage with us."

"Refused?"

"Declined, opted out, and chose not to. Said he didn't want to publicly contradict hospital policy."

"That doesn't sound so bad."

"I know, I know," said Joan. "It's just the way he goes about it. So smug. That superior attitude, it really is hateful. To me, anyway. He's always on the attack, always critical, and always so self-assured."

"Sounds like this puppy has been peeing on your lamp post."

"It's more than that, wise guy. You should have seen the look he gave me when I said this infant could be in terrible pain. It was creepy, sometimes he scares me. I can't have a five-minute conversation with him without fearing he will bring up the abortion issue."

"Sounds creepy. Joan."

I just don't like him, Alan. Don't like his views, don't like him, and don't trust him. He is a walking, talking dichotomy. On the one hand, he won't be part of the press conference. On the other, he agrees to take the case and then offers to pay for the child's funeral. Does that sound like the first thing a pro-life wacko would do? Put up the money for a funeral? Fedderson says he's done it before. And it's best that I simply ignore him. He's up to something, and I'm going to find out what."

"So he's camera shy and he pays funeral expenses for his patients. I like that policy. More doctors should pay for patient funerals. That's one way to reduce malpractice insurance costs. But, honestly, Joan, what could he be up to, and what are you going to do, snoop around his office? I'm a lawyer, but criminal law is not my specialty. Keep your distance. Don't go poking around in his business."

"No, nothing like that. I'm just going to notice what he's up to. I'm going to pay attention, ask a few questions, and look into a couple of things. He's up to something."

"I'm up to something too," said Alan turning the living room light off. "Are you going to investigate me?"

"As a matter of fact, I intend to conduct a thorough search tonight. Come here."

CHAPTER 4

Two weeks following the press conference Fedderson called for a 9 a.m. meeting in his office to bring the doctors up to date on the search to find a family member.

"Glad you could all make it," said Fedderson. "Vivian was supposed to be here too, but I've gone over most of this material with her so we can get started. I guess the first place to begin is to let you know that no one claiming to be a relative or even friend of Ms. Franco's has yet contacted the hospital. A number of leads -- people who say she looks like someone who once lived across the street, or who used to work at the mall, that sort of thing--are being tracked by the local police and the county's sheriff's department. But since no crime has been committed, this case is not necessarily their top priority, so even that has been slow going. We do know a couple of things. Ms. Franco does not have a criminal record; nor was she in the U.S. military, or a Federal employee. The FBI was unable to find a matching set of fingerprints in their files."

"There must be a record of her somewhere," said Dr. Tully. "What about her social security number?"

"Through the IRS the police were able to trace her work history. Her employment record is spotty, a year here, eight months there, then four or five months with no record of employment or any indication that she collected unemployment. At times, she may have had jobs off the books, was paid under the table, in cash. She had lousy jobs with lousy companies. From tax withholding records the police can figure out where and when she worked for a paycheck. Then they can interview employees to get some information on our mystery woman. There's a lot of work involved, this case isn't the highest priority for the police. This process could take a lot of time and yield nothing."

"You wouldn't think that someone could be so anonymous today. You can't go to the grocery store without having to give up your name and phone number," said Tully.

"You can't if you are in the mainstream economy. Every day we use credit cards, checks, ATM cards. Details about our whole lives are in computer files kept by banks and credit card companies. Even Facebook has a dossier on everyone."

"Be that as it may," interrupted Fedderson, "our young patient lived on the periphery of the economic mainstream, no credit cards, no loans, no credit history. From what we could tell she lived a life on the economic edge, below the poverty line, just a few hundred dollars ahead of being homeless, in many ways a typical American."

"What about her driver's license?" asked Tully.

"Another dead end. She got her driver's license, her first Pennsylvania license anyway, within the last year and lists her current address," said Fedderson. "The point is, she wasn't renewing an older license with another address on it, and she wasn't transferring a license from another state."

"And her car?" asked Tully.

"A '98 Toyota Corolla, bought for cash from a used car lot in Hawley a week after she got her license. Didn't take much cash either as you can imagine."

"So what about the calls that have come in, any leads?" asked Dr. Evans.

"As you know, the first two days the calls just swamped the switchboard. I should have realized that might happen. Anyway, we are averaging about 275 calls a day.

"And the results?" asked Evans.

"Better than two thirds of the calls are offers to donate money. Separate funds have been started to benefit the mother and the child," said Fedderson.

"Why separate?" asked Dr. Evans.

"A surprising number of persons making donations

want the money to go to the child, not the mother. So we had to set up two funds. Of the $33,750 collected, better than $24,000 is earmarked for the baby."

"Why the baby and not the mother?" asked Tully.

"We don't ask," said Fedderson, "but it appears that most people consider the infant to be totally blameless in this, a complete innocent."

"Can't argue with that," said Evans.

"...but some people tend to blame the mother."

"For what?" asked Evans.

"Who knows," said Fedderson, "for being a single mother, for being a bad driver, for being out late at night, any number of prejudiced reasons."

"It amazes me how some people are able to manage being vindictive while engaging in what should be a purely charitable act," said Evans.

"So what happens with the money?" asked Tully.

"Nothing. We keep good records, and if either becomes a ward of the state or a relative steps forward we deal with the disbursement then," said Fedderson.

"So, there are no good leads on family or friends," said Evans.

"Not a one," responded Fedderson. "However, there have been three marriage proposals."

"People are getting weirder all the time," said Evans.

"Perhaps not as weird as you might guess," Tully offered.

Evans and Fedderson turned to Tully.

"What, what are you saying," Evans asked.

"We've been running an EEG every 48 hours. Based on this morning's scan, it appears Ms. Franco has shown some improvement."

"Improvement?" questioned Evans.

"Indeed," said Tully, "based on the current level of brain activity, I would now describe her condition as, well, there is improvement, slight but not insignificant. Her vital signs, brain functioning, all the dials are up."

"I don't know whether to laugh or cry," joked Evans.

"Let's wait a few days. I'll keep you informed as the readings are evaluated."

"For how long?" asked Fedderson. "How long can she hold on?"

"Right now the question of irreversible coma is greatly diminished. We have to wait. Yes, she could suffer a series of strokes which could, at the worst case, be fatal. But the result could have an uglier result..."

"Are you saying she could be 'brain dead'?"

"A lot is going on, Doug. But, yes, that is another possible outcome."

"Long term care," Fedderson responded.

"There have been cases of braid-dead patients breathing on their own for ten years," said. Evans.

"Ten years!" said Fedderson. "She might remain in this condition for ten more years?"

"I want to remind you that she is in a coma, not brain dead. And recovery is possible," said Tully. "So far I like the results that I see. But, there is not much more we can do to prevent further strokes. She is receiving all the proper meds to help her brain strengthen. And she is young and strong...that matters."

"But, if she lingers on," said Evans, "and no relative is available to advise us as to treatment, the hospital could go to court to discontinue treatment."

"I don't like the sound of that," said Fedderson.

"This is one of those cases," said Evans, "that make you realize how sensible a living will is. But at this time there is not much chance of this patient having an attorney to take care of such matters."

"Speaking of lawyers, where the hell is Vivian?" said Fedderson.

As if on cue the phone rang. Fedderson picked up the receiver.

"Doug, its Vivian."

"We were just wondering where you are. Dr. Tully has been giving us the latest news about Ms. Franco, who appears is rallying."

"You'll understand why I missed it when I tell you who I've been talking to," said Vivian.

"And that is..."

"An attorney who claims to represent Ms. Franco's common-law husband and father of the baby girl."

CHAPTER 5

Two days later, Vivian Modell and Doug Fedderson sat in her office while nervously discussing the case while awaiting the arrival of Steve Williams, the man who claimed to be the father of Janice Franco's daughter. His attorney, Sidney Armstadt, would accompany Mr. Williams.

According to Vivian, Armstadt was a hustling attorney who specialized in defending DUI cases. "He even charges for the initial consultation," she offered.

"That's how he met Mr. Williams," said Vivian. "Apparently, Williams went to Armstadt for help. Their first meeting was after our press conference and Williams brought up the issue."

"So what's the consensus on Armstadt? Are we dealing with some sleaze ball shyster?" asked Fedderson.

"My goodness, such language in referring to a member of the Bar in good standing," Vivian smiled.

"You know what I mean, is this guy a shark or what?"

"He's not a superstar, according to the people I spoke with. He does a good job for his clients. The perception is that he has a fairly high success rate."

"You have to love the law," said Fedderson. "Putting drunks back on the road is seen as a good thing."

"Blame it on the Constitution's Bill of Rights. Those pesky impediments to law enforcement like prohibiting unreasonable search and seizure and requiring police to have probable cause before they pull us over. By the way, dear, I've noticed lately that you seem to have a thing about lawyers, a profession to which, you would do well to remember, I belong."

"I admit only a thing for one attorney, counselor," said Fedderson, smiling. "But I am worried about this setup. Why does the father need an attorney? Does this guy smell a big fee? What model of car does he drive?"

"Why can't you believe that he's just representing the best interests of his client? The client is in trouble; the attorney is there to protect the client's interests. The client has this other issue which as far as he or the attorney knows, could create a financial burden on the client. Maybe he wants to see his daughter; maybe he wants to see Ms. Franco. This man might be motivated out of love."

"Love does not require an attorney."

"Love may not, but your immediate love life does, so watch what you say about the members of my esteemed profession."

"I offer a complete apology," said Fedderson, standing up so he could bow with great flourish. "Please tell me what I can do to make amends."

"I'll consider your offer. We'll work out the details later," laughed Vivian as the phone rang. "That's probably them," she said, picking up the phone. "Yes, Tracy, fine. I'll be right out." Vivian hung up the phone, turned to Fedderson and stood up, saying, "Ready, sport? Our guests have arrived. Let's go see what this shyster and his scumbag client want of us poor upholders of truth, decency, and the American Way. And, if you don't mind, let me do most of the talking once we get past the pleasantries."

"You're the lawyer," said Fedderson, crossing in front of Vivian to open the door leading from her office to the plush lobby.

"Vivian Modell," said Vivian, offering her hand to the short, impeccably dressed man with a well-used leather briefcase.

"Sidney Armstadt," said the man. "A pleasure to meet you, a genuine pleasure. And this is Mr. Williams," he said, turning to the tall heavyset man, who managed to look like a bouncer in a bar on the rough side of town even though he was wearing a new sports jacket, crisp new slacks, bright yellow shirt, and complementary silk tie. He was someone for whom a

51

jacket and tie were a decidedly new, uncomfortable, and unwelcome experience. Vivian guessed that Armstadt had Williams buy the clothes for his DUI court appearance and made him wear them to this meeting as well.

Williams did not look into Vivian's eyes as he offered his hand and mumbled, "Pleasure."

"And this is Mr. Doug Fedderson, the hospital administrator," said Vivian, pausing as the men shook hands. "And of course you met Tracy earlier. She holds this place together." Tracy Evers, an attractive 23-year-old redhead smiled as the men nodded to her. Her conservative blue blazer, white blouse, and blue skirt could not disguise a body that, as Greg, the newest law clerk in the firm was wont to say, would not quit. Tracy was attractive. This fact had not been lost on Williams, who leisurely, but constantly, eyed her from head to toe.

Tracy did not react to the stare. Such looks were a part of her life, unwelcome, unappreciated, and all too common for her to bother with, especially within the confines of the office, where she did not feel she had the freedom to openly challenge or admonish visitors and clients. To herself she correctly labeled him a 'loser.'

But Williams's lewd stare was not lost on Vivian, whose initial mild distaste for Mr. Williams was building into a strong dislike.

"Before we go into my office," said Vivian, "would anyone care for something to drink? Coffee, soda, juice?"

"None for me, nothing, thanks, nothing," said Armstadt.

"You got diet Coke?" asked Williams.

"I'm certain we do," answered Vivian. "Tracy, a diet Coke for Mr. Williams. Mr. Fedderson, anything for you? No. Well then, Tracy, if you don't mind, an orange juice for me. We'll be in my office. Please hold all my calls until we're done. Gentlemen, shall we adjourn to my office?"

Vivian directed the men to be seated at the small

conference table in the corner of the spacious office.

Williams looked around. "This is nice," he said. "Big. Bigger even than yours, Sid. And the plants are real, and flowers, too."

"Ah, well," said Vivian, "that's the difference in the cost of office space in rural Wayne County and Philadelphia. You're in the big leagues there, the majors."

"Yes, the majors, the Eagles and Phillies. And my office is just seven miles from Center City. Sounds further than it is," said Armstadt. "All of the problems, none of the glamour, however. This is a very nice office, yes, very nice. Beautiful, nice flowers."

Tracy delivered the diet Coke and orange juice, much to the pleasure of Williams, who continued to stare at her until she left the room. Vivian had decided that Mr. Williams was not acting like a man who was terribly upset to learn his infant daughter was terminally ill and his former lover was severely injured.

"Well," said Vivian. "How shall we start? What would you like to accomplish during this meeting, Mr. Armstadt?"

"As you know," said Armstadt, straightening up in his chair, "this is a very tragic situation for all concerned. The mother, the child, my client—tragic," he sympathized as he cleaned his trifocal glasses with the pocket square he removed from his light gray suit jacket.

"A painful situation for all," said Vivian.

"For all," said Fedderson.

"And a difficult situation for the hospital as well, I'm sure," said Armstadt.

"The hospital's situation pales beside the human tragedy," said Fedderson.

"Yes, yes, of course," said Armstadt, beginning to speak a little more quickly, "but still, there are considerations, practical considerations that, well, I would be unfair to my client if I did not watch out for his interests..."

"Of course..." said Vivian.

"These practical considerations could have a deleterious effect, very bad, on the financial well-being of Mr. Williams here, who, I'm sure he would not mind my revealing this--we've spoken about it, discussed it in detail--is a man of limited means. Limited. He now finds himself, through no fault of his own, finds himself in this tragic situation with no familial support at all, none."

"Janice has no family, then," said Vivian addressing Williams as he sipped the soda.

"Not as far as I know," said Williams. "We talked a couple of times about it. She didn't say much. Said she was an only child. I asked her about her parents. 'They're dead,' she said and I asked 'When did they die?' And she'd got all pissed off and said, 'Not soon enough,' and then she told me to get off it. What was I to do? So, I'm it, no family."

"And you're certain that Ms. Franco is the woman you, ah, knew?" asked Fedderson.

"I should hope to tell ya. Yeah, I'm sure. You can't get something like that wrong. I've got pictures of us together. Mr. Armstadt has them."

"Not with me today, didn't bring them today, but he gave me pictures," said Armstadt. "He and Ms. Franco. The two of them. Attractive couple. All smiles. Such a shame really, a shame."

"So how long were you together?" asked Vivian.

"I don't know, what, 18 months, almost two years, a while. I'm not good with anniversaries and things. Janice was always counting that stuff like it mattered. Months together, six months since our first date, a month since our first fight. To me, we were just together, you know, the time didn't matter. We were together, that was it. We were together today so what did it matter that we were together yesterday too. Women are always into counting weeks and months and celebrating this date and that date. It never made sense to me."

"Did you have what you would call a commitment, were you soul mates, did you talk about marriage?" asked

Vivian.

Williams looked as if he was about to answer. But then his eyes widened and he got an odd look on his face. He cleared his throat instead of speaking. Vivian knew that Armstadt had just deliberately stepped on Williams's foot. Admitting that the couple intended to get married would help establish a claim of common law marriage and Armstadt was not yet ready to concede that point.

"Before we fully explore the nature of their relationship, these questions are, after all, difficult for my client under these circumstances, difficult circumstances. Would you mind if we discussed some of the practical matters we had referenced earlier?"

"By all means. Ask anything you like," said Vivian.

"Thank you, Vivian, thank you so much. Now, then, Mr. Fedderson..."

"Yes..."

"Do you have a feel, do you know the, ah, costs of care to date? For the child. The mother is another matter, another matter. I know these things are difficult to estimate, so many variables, so many. I don't envy you your job. Very difficult. All that accounting, so many spread sheets, all those columns with sub-totals. But you must have a sense, an order of magnitude you understand, for how much it costs to care for the child. Order of magnitude. A ballpark figure, per day, you understand, ballpark figure."

It was Vivian's turn to step on Fedderson's toes. He looked at her quizzically.

"We don't have the numbers with us right now," said Vivian.

"Order of magnitude, educated guess, that's all. Educated guess," said Armstadt.

"Well, I'm not really comfortable providing an educated guess when Mr. Fedderson would be able to give you a very accurate response in a few days. Actually, this level of detail in our discussions should probably wait until we have confirmation that Mr. Williams is the father of the infant."

"What are you trying to say," said Williams, taking offense at Vivian's statement.

"Just a formality, Mr. Williams, isn't that right, Mr. Armstadt, just a formality," said Vivian pointedly adopting Armstadt's habit of redundant phrasing. "For your own good, and for the protection of the hospital, for everyone involved, everyone, we must first establish you are the biological father."

"Yes, yes, of course, a necessary step. Necessary. Have to. Even though, with the photos and all, I have no doubt in the matter, no doubt you understand. None. Still, faith isn't evidence, is it, Ms. Modell? Not evidence. Not at all. Naturally, a blood test is required and DNA match, of course. I had considered having it done prior to our meeting, but thought better of it. Thought I'd save the hospital some money by paying for it myself, a gesture of my, ah, our goodwill, our best intentions. I am assuming the hospital would prefer to conduct its own test. Less room for doubt. No room for doubt I dare say. None."

"What's this blood test stuff?" demanded Williams squirming in his chair. "Do I have to do anything? I already told you we were together. What more do you need?"

"It's a simple matter. We'll need a blood sample," said Vivian, "and your permission to match it with a sample from the baby. And the DNA test is simply a cotton swab swished in your mouth. Technology takes it from there. Very simple, a normal procedure."

"Oh man, I hate needles," said Williams. "Do we haffta do this? And that cotton swab thing!"

"A necessary step, Mr. Williams," said Armstadt confidently. "Completely necessary. But not painful, a little discomfort, over in a minute. Less than a minute. Half a minute, perhaps even less, several seconds, maybe."

"If I gotta…" muttered Williams shaking his head.

"Very good then," said Armstadt, "but before we take that step we'd like a formal agreement, something in writing, indicating that my client, if paternity can be established, is not liable for any or all of the costs incurred or about to be incurred for the care and treatment of either Ms. Franco or the infant. They were not living together at the time of her accident, the car going off the road."

"Is it your position, Mr. Armstadt, that your client is indigent?"

"Limited resources, very limited. No assets. Car, job, apartment, debt. Far lesser burdens would force him into bankruptcy, far lesser," said Armstadt. "We have prepared a financial statement that I would be willing to share with you. Did it myself, all the numbers you need in one place, very neat."

"The hospital's position is that the father, if indigent, is not liable for those costs. Lake Veterans Memorial is a compassionate hospital," said Vivian smiling.

"We can show he is indigent now. Easy to do. Easy. But what if he comes into money in the future?"

"Expecting to cash in on something soon?" asked Vivian.

"Must protect my client," said Armstadt. "His parents are getting along, seemingly healthy but who knows? He may have a small inheritance coming. Wouldn't want to see it go to pay for hospital bills after he came forward and all. An honest man. Hardly seems fair."

"And he might win the lottery," said Vivian.

"Within the realm of possibility," said Armstadt, "within the realm of possibility if he had the resources to purchase a chance. Money being tight. So then, should my client come into money in the future, would the hospital make any claim upon it?"

"Well, Mr. Armstadt, if he did, say, win a few million in the lottery, don't you think he should pay something?" said Fedderson.

"I see your point," said Armstadt, "but what if he wins $100,000, should all of that be used to settle these medical bills?"

"I'm sure we can work out an arrangement," said Vivian, "whereby if Mr. Williams's net worth is less than $300,000 for the next three years, the hospital will make no claim upon him. After three years the hospital will make no claim on him no matter what his net worth. If he discovers oil in his backyard and becomes filthy rich, it's all his after the three year period."

"It is a good concept," said Armstadt, "very good. It would, of course need to be adjusted here and there. Time and inflation, you understand. The devil's in the details. In the details. So if we tweaked the concept a bit, say, tweaked the net worth ceiling to $750,000…"

"I don't see why we couldn't…" began Fedderson.

"Mr. Fedderson, if you don't mind, I don't think we should rush into this," said Vivian.

"You're the lawyer," said Fedderson.

"Mr. Armstadt," said Vivian looking straight at him, "what would you say if we agreed that we won't seek any money from Mr. Williams in the next three years if his net worth does not go above $350,000?"

"I would say $500, 000," said Armstadt. "A more reasonable figure."

"And my final response would be $400,000, Mr. Armstadt," said Vivian.

"In writing?" said Armstadt. "Just a formality, you understand, another formality."

"If you'd like to work out the details this afternoon," said Vivian, "we could have a letter of agreement ready tomorrow morning."

"To show our good faith," said Armstadt, "we'll go to the hospital today and have the blood withdrawn and swab the inner cheek. One quick sweep," he motioned looking at his client. "Tomorrow we'll return here, review the letter of agreement and if all is in order we'll sign the letter and then sign whatever release forms you deem are necessary to complete our agreement and demonstrate our goodwill. How's that? Everyone's interests are protected, and we don't lose any time. No undue delays. None. Done, lickety split!"

"Sounds like a plan to me," said Vivian. "I'll dictate the statement to Tracy for Doug's signature, and Doug, would you mind calling the hospital to arrange for Mr. Williams to give us a blood sample?" she said looking for agreement at all concerned. "OK then, I'll call Tracy in. I think we are on our way to resolving what is a very difficult situation."

"Tragic, truly tragic," said Armstadt as Williams eagerly watched the doorway waiting for Tracy to re-enter the room.

Ten minutes later Armstadt and Williams left Vivian's office and were on their way to Lake Veterans Hospital.

The two men were silent until they were at the attorney's leased Mercedes Benz. Armstadt felt confident about the meeting. It went more smoothly than the imagined. He felt satisfied that Williams conducted himself with honor and integrity. "A good day," he thought.

"So, what do you think we can get out of them? Fifty grand? Can we get fifty grand?" asked Williams eagerly.

"Please, Mr. Williams," said the attorney. "I've told you before, these are very delicate matters. Very delicate. We need to approach this carefully, tactfully. Very tactfully."

"I didn't say anything wrong in there. Just like you said. I didn't mention money. I let you do all the money talking."

"You did very well, very well indeed. Now, did you notice I was asking them questions about the cost of the care? Did you notice? Per diem cost for the child, daily expenses for her care."

"Yeah."

"That's the key to what we can get from them. The key. If it costs $1000 a day to care for her, and believe me that's not out of the question. Not out of the question at all. That would be $365,000 per year. So how long will the child live, how long will the hospital have her in their charge? It's not how much we think they might have to spend, they won't respond based on that. Won't respond at all. But how much do they believe, or fear, fear is a very powerful motivator, very powerful, how much do they fear it will cost them to care for this child? These are bean counters, bean counters. They don't like the unknown. Rather have a hard and fast figure. Something they can budget for. That's the margin of opportunity for us. We find out what they fear this is going to cost them and we offer them a clean way out for half that price. It's a good deal for them, great deal. Nice, neat, and clean. They are off the hook; we've done a public service by giving them a way not to have to spend all that money on a hopeless case, hopeless. Well, we're here," announced Armstadt, carefully steering the Mercedes into the hospital parking lot.

"This better not hurt."

"As I said, slight discomfort. Very slight, I'm told. Very slight. Now while we are here we must ask for permission to see the mother and the baby," said Armstadt.

"What for?"

"Must ask. It is only right. Father would want to see the child, the mother. They'd expect it, you know."

"Yeah, well this father doesn't want to see the kid. On the news they say she's all wired up with tubes. Who needs to see that? As for that bitch of a mother, I couldn't care less what happens to her after the stuff she pulled..."

"Don't worry, they probably won't let you see either of them until the results of the blood test are in and prove you're the father. Still, we must ask. It's expected of us. A small price to pay considering the potential payoff. Small price."

***

Three days later, shortly after arriving at his office, Dr. Frederick Nichols received a call from Doug Fedderson.

"Got plans for lunch today?" asked Fedderson.

"Let's see," said Nichols, checking the appointment calendar, "I'm fee as a bird from 12:30 to 1:45. What's up?"

"Need to go over a few things regarding the Baby Franco case..."

"Blood tests are in then..."

"Yeah, Williams is the father. Conclusive results."

"Can't this poor baby catch a break?"

"Were you really expecting a candidate for 'Father of the Year'?"

"No, I guess not. Well, the father is the father. Any idea of what he intends to do?"

"That's the topic for lunch. Vivian will be joining us, if you don't mind?"

"Not at all."

"OK, we'll meet at Zimmerman's. We've got a table reserved in the back and can go over everything. My treat."

"Oh, oh, lunch with you and an attorney and you're buying, that's ominous. Last time you bought... come to think of it, the next time you buy lunch, this will be the last time you bought lunch."

"You have a very selective memory, Doctor, but the invitation still stands. Is 12:30 OK?"

"I'll be there."

Shortly before 12:30, Dr. Nichols parked his leased Passat next to Fedderson's BMW in Zimmerman's parking lot. Recognizing him as her obstetrician, the restaurant hostess chatted with him for a bit before leading him to Fedderson's table at the far end of the sparsely populated dining room. Fedderson rose and offered his hand to Nichols. "Glad you could make it, Fred," said Fedderson.

"Good to see you, Dr. Nichols," said Vivian.

The trio made themselves comfortable and ordered light drinks from the waitress who handed them each a daily special menu and a smile.

"So, Doug, you indicated you had some idea of the father's intentions."

"Yes, Vivian and I think we have an inkling of what he and his attorney may want."

"What's the deal with the attorney? Why is he necessary?"

"That's the disturbing part of this," said Fedderson.

"I'm listening," said Dr. Nichols.

"What would you do if the father requested that we modify treatment for the infant?" asked Vivian.

Nichols sat silent. He sipped the water had waitress had served. "Modify treatment?"

"We're a small hospital in rural Pennsylvania. More relaxed than the big cities. Able to jostle more."

"With the same ethics, the same access to treatment, the same highly trained physicians, you want to add to your disqualifier," Nichols quickly interjected. "Steel yourself," he thought. "This is what it is all about."

He began, "I'd have two basic choices, accede to those wishes or withdraw from the case."

"I understand, but in this case, what would you do?"

"You know I favor continued treatment, but if the family makes--and I know that talk like this drives some of my fellow physicians crazy--but if the family makes what I consider a spiritually valid decision, I could concur with a decision to withdraw treatment that, even in my judgment was preventing death rather than sustaining life."

"Is that a possibility in this case?"

"Well, Doug, based on what you and Vivian have told me about the father, let's just say I would be surprised, and delighted of course, if he were able to arrive at what I would consider a spiritually informed decision."

"I understand," said Vivian. "But what about the treatment merely delaying death rather than sustaining life? Could you support withdrawal of treatment on that basis, even if the father's reasoning might not be up to your standards?"

"Under certain circumstances, yes. I mean, if a

patient is brain dead, a totally flat line, and the only thing keeping the body from decomposing is medical machinery forcing the heart to beat and pushing air into the lungs, that sort of thing. In my mind, the body has died; the machinery is just getting in the way of the totally natural process..."

"Might that occur here?"

"It might. But it hasn't yet, and until it does, I insist we continue treatment. Based on your comments, may I assume you expect the father to request we withdraw treatment, that we modify treatment, am I correct?"

"We do, but it's more than that," said Fedderson.

The conversation stopped as the waitress delivered lunch to the table. When she left, Dr. Nichols resumed.

"Are we back to the attorney then...?" he asked.

"Now this is confidential," said Vivian.

"OK, Doug."

"This attorney, well, he strikes me as a real sleaze ball..."

"This is the big news; a Philadelphia lawyer is a snake..."

"There are snakes and there are snakes. Some are harmless, and then there are water moccasins..."

"Still, a Philadelphia lawyer who is a nasty snake, we haven't broken new ground yet."

"Vivian thinks they are going to ask for money as a *quid pro quo* for discontinuing treatment," said Fedderson.

Dr. Nichols blinked once, put his fork down and pushed his Caesar salad aside but said nothing.

"Doug's right," said Vivian. "I believe they want money in return for authorizing us to discontinue treatment."

"How...?"

"They won't come out and make a formal request," said Fedderson.

"Not in so many words," added Vivian. "They'll do it indirectly, perhaps through the hospital's insurance carrier."

"With this lawyer, it just might be direct," Nichols

offered. "But, you can't be considering such an agreement..."

"Hear us out, Doctor," said Vivian. "We're telling you this because we understand your strong religious convictions might put you in conflict with official hospital policy. We want you to know the full story. Doug may not have any control over the situation if the insurance company gets involved."

"Doug, you're the hospital administrator..."

"I will of course do what I can," said Fedderson.

"Dr. Nichols," said Vivian, "let me tell you how I think things might develop. Remember, I only suspect that the father and attorney are out for money. They have not said anything specific yet."

"But you believe they will."

"We believe so," said Fedderson.

"Based on what?"

"Armstadt has given me a list of questions," said Vivian. "We offered to sign an agreement stating that the father was not responsible for any of the costs of care in this case, after receiving a financial statement indicating the father is indigent."

"Let me guess. He's not in the same bracket with Donald Trump," said Nichols. "Oh, I don't mean to get political. Just a figure of speech, an example," he smiled.

"Correct. Makes enough to live on, food, shelter, beer, not necessarily in that order."

"So it's legitimate, he can't pay for treatment, and we gave or will give, the lawyer a statement saying the father is not liable for any costs," said Dr. Nichols.

"Right," said Fedderson. "But here's the kicker. Armstadt has insisted that the hospital not go after Williams if he comes into a windfall during the next few years."

"I don't understand."

"OK," said Vivian, "We've got Williams, living paycheck to paycheck. But his attorney negotiated a deal with the hospital that prevents us from forcing him to pay any of these medical expenses so long as his net worth does not exceed $400,000."

"So, what are the chances of that?" said Dr. Nichols.

"That's just it, Fred," said Fedderson. "You wouldn't think there was any chance for this character to increase his net worth above a six pack. But Armstadt apparently thinks the guy is coming into some money. And he had an inordinate interest in the past and future cost of care for Janice Franco and the baby."

"I think," said Vivian, "they may be preparing a pitch that goes like this: There's $14,000 that has been donated for the mother and the nearly $40,000 sent in for the baby's care.

She paused. "Williams and Armstadt have shoved their faces in front of every camera from Honesdale to Scranton to Timbuktu. From his TV interviews you can just sense that there isn't a deep well of paternal love in this man. He comes off as cold and unfeeling, an opportunist, even when he talks about the terrible tragedy. Just doesn't ring true. And Armstadt—David Copperfield's Uriah Heep has charisma to spare compared to Armstadt."

"Evil can't be masked," said Dr. Nichols. "The world's misfortune is that we accept evil, even while recognizing it. It's become cultural white noise."

"I don't know about evil, but these two give me the creeps," said Vivian. "Anyway, the donated money will probably go to the hospital to create a special indigents' fund or some other approved designated trust, or perhaps go directly to the insurance carrier. Whatever amount the hospital directly receives for providing the Franco's hospital care, the insurance company won't duplicate. It's like the United Way campaign. If an individual directly gives to a United Way campaign charity via paycheck donation $100, then the United Way subtracts that amount from the planned giving amount it had in its budget for the charity. The charity or the hospital in this case doesn't receive double the amount," she explained. "Is everyone with me?"

Nichols nodded and Fedderson smiled.

Vivian continued. "So, again, what the insurance company receives will go to the hospital in the form of disbursement for expenses. There is no increase in income for the hospital. Now, the hospital, according to latest figures, spends about $1,000., above the insurance rate," she emphasized, "on the infant patient. Physician costs and even an additional modicum of special care treatments would increase that figure, but let's just consider hospital costs for purposes of discussion. And we expect her to live how long...?"

Dr. Nichols paused and shifted in his chair before answering. "In her condition, it's day-to-day. She could last 18 months, she could die tonight. She's in a weakened condition; the hospital has plenty of airborne contagions around. She could develop pneumonia, a staph infection, or any of her major organs might shut down at any time. Your guess is as good as mine. Medicine can do only so much."

"If I asked you for your best estimate..."

Dr. Nichols paused, and stared intently at Fedderson before answering.

"In the hospital environment, I'd give her six months, max, with the understanding that she could go at any time. The odds of additional life-threatening conditions developing are very high if she remains in the hospital for the next six months. There is another scenario..."

"And that is..."

"Adequate care outside of the hospital environment, a private setting removed from the high incidence of threatening germs. She might live for years, live out her natural life, God's plan for all of us."

"The hospital does not see that as an option," said Vivian. "And who is to say that another environment, a different location is more germ-free than Lake Veterans!"

"It's amazing! Hubris is alive and kicking in the species called homo sapiens! How important we humans believe we are to the world order to so confidently say God's plan is not an option, not God's plan but my plan."

It's easy to see why this guy gets under Dr. Evans's skin, thought Vivian before responding to Dr. Nichols. "As I understand free will, Doctor, that is exactly the power God granted mankind," said Vivian. "Free will and pride might be several of the characteristics of being fully human. But please, I don't want this to become a religious debate. Knowing your strong beliefs, Doug thought it best that we review the hospital's position with you. He wanted you to be aware of what might be developing."

"I wanted you to have a chance to prepare yourself," said Fedderson.

Dr. Nichols gave Fedderson a knowing look. "And I thank you for that. So tell me, Vivian. Why can't the hospital take action to assure God the Father's will be done in this matter?"

"Because the father, that's father with a small 'f'," said Vivian, "won't allow it and, as the biological father, he has the legal authority to approve treatment. There's something called 'parental rights' that's headlining this case."

"The hospital could fight it," countered Dr. Nichols.

"On what grounds," asked Vivian? "The father's request is well within existing case law. Whatever our personal convictions we must follow the law."

"There is civil disobedience," said Dr. Nichols. "This could be an opportunity for the hospital to take a courageous stand in favor of life. Doug, think of what that could do for the hospital."

"Dr. Nichols," said Vivian before Fedderson could respond, "You are being unreasonable. As a matter of policy, the hospital does not share your social agenda. Breaking the law to further your religious beliefs is simply not an option for the hospital. In addition I don't think the hospital wants battling picket lines walking the street in front of the hospital, like that case in New Jersey some years back."

"As offensive as some of these proposals may be to us," said Fedderson, "my job imposes certain obligations on me that…"

""Those secular obligations pale when compared to our obligations to God," said Dr. Nichols.

Vivian sighed at the comment. Fedderson said nothing.

"So," continued Nichols, "where does that leave us? I suppose if I refuse to follow the father's wishes I would be removed from the case."

"Certainly," said Vivian. "Even if the hospital didn't remove you, Armstadt could get a court order within hours. And then there's the matter of the insurance company."

"Lawyers and insurance companies, why did we ever become doctors…"

"Necessary evils…" said Fedderson.

"Well, Doug, I agree with half of that assessment, I just don't think they are necessary."

"Nonetheless," said Fedderson, "let's say the insurance company agrees with you and anticipates this infant will survive in the hospital environment for six months, make it 200 days so the math is easy, at the arguably low insurance rate of $600 per day, that's $120,000. And the hospital eats the rest. Add another $200,000 to the bill! The father, through the honorable Mr. Armstadt, proposes to the insurance company that they will authorize discontinuing treatment immediately if…"

"If what?" demanded Nichols.

"If the insurance company agrees to pay, say $60,000 to the soon to be grieving father."

"Blood money…" said Nichols darkly.

"From our perspective, perhaps," said Vivian. "But to the insurance company, it's an opportunity to save $60,000. And who would argue with a decision that also relieves a young baby from a life of pain?"

"Doug, Vivian, I know you both. You can't be considering this."

"If it were our choice," said Fedderson, "we'd never agree to that deal. But understand, once the insurance company is involved, it might be out of my control."

"And you think the insurance company might actually consider doing this?"

"Dr. Nichols," said Fedderson, "as a doctor you know that insurance companies sometimes adopt a bottom line mentality that blinds them to any other consideration. They've proven that thousands of times with curtailment of funding procedures that treat 'orphan diseases' and certain medical treatment to elderly patients. Try getting a routine PSA test approved for a 71-year-old, and I could cite example after example. So, the unofficial-official hospital position would be to have the insurance company pay off these vermin once they give us permission to commit murder legally."

"Doctor," said Vivian, "I know this is upsetting for you. And while I would not characterize the situation in exactly those terms, I am sorry to say that you have the essentials right. The father agrees to withdraw treatment, the child dies, and the insurance company pays the father, Armstadt gets his cut and the hospital staff gets to return to real medicine."

"Doug," said Nichols, appealing directly to Fedderson, "you can't let this happen. You know I cannot be a party to this. I'd reject these instructions from loving parents, but from this opportunistic leech--It would be difficult for me to keep my composure."

"I'll make sure you two are never in the same room alone," said Fedderson. "I wish someone could do the same for me."

"Doctor, try to understand Doug's position. No matter how reprehensible this action is to him," said Vivian, "his official capacity obligates him to examine such options logically, unemotionally. He cannot operate this hospital on gut reactions, or his private version of morality."

"Vivian," said Dr. Nichols, "we have gut reactions for a reason. They warn of danger. We ignore those feelings at our peril. All too often those gut reactions are our conscience tugging at us to re-examine our situation and respond to it differently before a knee-jerk gut reaction."

"Well, Doctor," said Fedderson, "I don't know how much room I would have to maneuver once the insurance company is involved. I may not even be part of the decision."

"You can't wash your hands of it by saying the insurance company is at fault. I certainly won't. If it comes down to paying money to have the father terminate treatment, I would refuse to follow those instructions and I would do so publicly. If moral arguments don't move the insurance company, maybe publicity will."

"Doctor Nichols," said Vivian, "I seem to remember you giving your word you would not publicly go against hospital policy on this case."

"That was when hospital policy could claim some shred of decency; when it applied moral values to life-and-death decisions. That was when we had honest disagreements about medical and ethical issues. I never agreed to remain silent in the face of this non-medical, faceless, bottom-line immorality. What has been proposed is worse than extortion; it's murder for hire. It's the New York mob alive and willing in Honesdale. And they want the hospital to be the triggerman. I won't be a part of it. And don't even think about removing me from the case. You do and the *New York Times* gets an exclusive story from me."

"Well, Doctor," said Fedderson wearily, "I appreciate your candor. I really do. You have certainly given me a lot to think about."

"And you have given me much to pray about. Now, if you'll excuse me, I've got rounds to complete."

"Certainly, Doctor, I understand," said Fedderson. "Thank you for joining us."

Nichols abruptly left the table. Fedderson and Modell sat silently as the angry Dr. Nichols brusquely left the restaurant.

"Dr. Evans is right. He is a tiresome ideologue," said Vivian.

"A man with strong beliefs," countered Doug.

"Strong beliefs and no room for compromise. A dangerous combination. For him the sky is the limit."

"I know his beliefs run counter to yours, Viv…"

"That's got nothing to do with it. It's his inflexibility that gets to me. It's impractical, maybe even self-destructive. On a good day I can understand his obstinacy. We live our lives learning what's black and what's white. That's basically the formation of our conscience. But being a responsible decision-making adult means we understand the gray areas in life and being mature adults we realize we need to compromise within the gray areas. That's what makes progress. He doesn't understand that. He doesn't know what being responsible means."

"I understand your train of thought. But let's not argue about Dr. Nichols," said Doug. "I'm just saying he's got his good points."

"If you don't want to argue about Dr. Nichols," Vivian replied, "I suggest you stop defending the bastard."

"I'm not defending him, although I would not characterize him as a bastard."

"No? How about fanatic?" challenged Vivian. "You have to admit he's a fanatic."

"He has strongly held beliefs and he lives by them."

"Beliefs he wants to impose on everyone. He's a fanatic. How can you not see that?"

"There are fanatics on both sides of this issue."

"So, what are you saying? I'm the fanatic because I don't agree with your Dr. Nuthatch Nichols," Vivian said

71

sharply while glaring at Fedderson, who silently returned her stare. "Or is it," she continued, "because I don't agree with you? Is that it, Doug? You buy in to his 'strongly held beliefs'. Is that it? Is that what this is all about?"

"Viv, we've had a rough couple of days here. We're both tired. Maybe we both need some time away from the job."

"I'm not much in the mood for a weekend getaway with you right at this moment," said Vivian.

"I'm not suggesting one," said Fedderson. In fact, that's my point."

"What is?"

"We both need a break from the job. Problem is, we are the job. Any time we spend together we'll end up talking about the hospital, or Franco, or Dr. Nichols, or Armstadt and Williams. We can't get away from this whole thing if we're together."

"So, you don't want to see me anymore."

"Nothing that drastic, Viv. I just think it might be better for both of us, better for our relationship, if we just took a couple of days off from each other. We'll see each other during working hours most days. We need a break from each other after work. I mean look at us sitting here arguing about Dr. Nichols. That's not like us."

"Hey, well. Yeah, I can see the sense in this," said Vivian. She was slightly confused by the sudden turn of events and she was hurt by Fedderson's suggestion. But she instinctively knew that she wouldn't mind having a few days away from Doug Fedderson. She was losing herself in the whirlwind politics that were shaping the days since the auto accident; events that she had little or no control of. She was uncomfortable with that. She was always the one in charge. She made the decision where she worked, the kind of law she practiced, even the extent and depth of her relationship with Doug. It was strictly on her terms. Now, she was realizing that she had little effect on his strong beliefs and she didn't like not being in control. But in reality, even before he spoke, she was considering limiting the amount of time she spent at the hospital. That was her way of being the "boss" in both the relationship and the job.

"We do seem to be getting on each other's nerves," she said thoughtfully before continuing in a very cheerful voice, "OK, see you at work. Don't worry about the check. I'll bill the hospital anyway."

"See you tomorrow, Viv," said Fedderson who was now a little confused by Vivian's cheerful manner.

"10 a.m. meeting. I'll be there," she said smiling.

As Doug left the restaurant and Vivian paid the tab with her Visa card, Dr. Nichols was pulling into the hospital parking lot. He spent the next several hours in the hospital library. Finally he went directly to the neonatal intensive care unit and examined Baby Franco. He sighed and made several notations to her chart and left. A few minutes later the attending nurse approached the bassinet, looked at the revised chart with Dr. Nichols' negative life signs medical notations and sadly shook her head. He scribbled his signature on the bottom and parenthetically added: "Its 8:14 a.m. and baby Franco is dying."

Dr. Nichols drove to a nearby Wal-Mart parking lot. He retrieved the burner phone from the glove box and dialed a number he had called only five times before in his medical career.

"It's time," he said. "I'll make the arrangements on this end."

The voice on the other end simply replied, "Thanks, Doug," then added, "Do you think it's time for a change?"

"I'll let you know," he slowly replied.

CHAPTER 6

Later that evening, Joan felt ill. At first she decided the upset stomach was due to her enjoying the leftover pork and sauerkraut dinner. But then the she felt a slight pressure in her chest. "Indigestion," she decided. She took two antacids. She recalled that same uneasiness several days earlier. She shrugged it off then but now, again? She took two more antacids. The chalkiness reminded her of the taste of the milk shakes in the early days of the Stop and Go Restaurant in nearby Wilkes-Barre. "Were they really 'milk shakes' or just 'some kind of non-dairy formulated shakes'," she wondered. The shakes at the time were cheap and tasted like an antacid. "Maybe they really were an antacid," she thought, "they were formulated to counteract the lousy burgers they served," she decided. She sat on a straight chair in the living room and turned on the TV. "Mindless distraction," she championed her decision. Shortly afterwards she started to experience jaw pain, more chest pain, and fatigue. She mumbled, "No, it can't be. Not now!" She yelped for her husband but by the time he arrived she grabbed her chest and collapsed on the sofa. He screamed her name as he was calling 911.

****

At 2 a.m.., some four hours after Dr. Joan Evans had her heart attack; Dr. Nichols was again at the side of his infant patient.

"It is better this way, after all," he said half-aloud as he carefully completed the hospital paperwork and patient chart. He then reached for a death certificate and hastily completed a diagnosis: Inclusion-cell disease-mucolipidosis…failure to thrive. He had contacted Grayson's Funeral Home shortly after arriving at the hospital a half-hour earlier.

"She must be picked up immediately," he told Avery Grayson. "If we delay the move from the morgue to the funeral home until tomorrow, there's too great a change that the newspapers might get wind of her death and swarm all over us."

Dr. Nichols waited at the side of baby Franco's bassinette until the van from Grayson's arrived. Avery carried what looked like a garment bag out of the back of the van and systematically yet ceremonially placed it on the gurney. He walked to the NICU and nodded to Nichols as he entered the "Parents Only" enclosure. He examined the paperwork without much conversation, and signed for the release. Satisfied, Nichols and Grayson ever so gently lifted the body and placed her in the bag. "Such an angel," Nichols commented. "Don't close the bag. Leave it open. Life is more dignified that way," he added. The walk to the van only took several minutes. Carefully, the funeral home gurney was placed in the rear of the van and the body secured. "I'll take good care of her," Grayson added. After the funeral van pulled away from the hospital, Nichols walked to his car.

****

The following morning, the hospital issued a terse press release:

Baby Franco has died. The child, called 'miracle-baby' by the hospital attending staff was born soon after an accident in which her mother lost control of her car and it skidded off Route 6 and crashed in the Lackawaxen River east of Honesdale. Janice Franco and her unnamed baby girl became the subject of many human interest stories. Moved by sympathy and civic pride a medical assistance fund was established to provide for her medical care. Her mother, Janice, remains in critical but stable condition at Lake Veterans Memorial Hospital and is showing signs of improvement. The child has been released to the Grayson Funeral Home. Further information will be made public as it becomes available.

75

As Dr. Nichols had predicted, the press swarmed on the hospital and the funeral home like locusts on a corn field once word of the baby's death was announced. The press' attention focused on the sad plight of a mother never having seen nor held her child. "How's the mother doing?" "Did she ever regain consciousness?" "Were mother and daughter in the same room at the time of the baby's death?" One questioner even asked if the mother breast fed the baby prior to her death.

Some questions swirled around the medical fund that was set up to pay for the baby's care. There was quite a bit of curiosity about the beneficiary of the trust. Some suggested the father receive the money, others the Grayson funeral home to provide a proper funeral. The fact that Joan Evans, the doctor who delivered baby Franco, suffered a heart attack and was admitted to the hospital was not of immediate interest nor barely noted by the press.

The death of the baby caught Armstadt off guard. He quickly phoned Williams informing and consoling him that his "baby girl had died." He suggested he take a cold shower to freshen up and get the cob webs out of his head and be ready to issue a press release within the hour. He again expressed his condolences while considering the next move. After all, he didn't come all this way to the "north woods of Pennsylvania" for nothing.

"An hour?" Williams questioned. "I can't be ready in an hour. Maybe two but not one." Armstadt agreed that two was better than one. "Must be the new math," he murmured to himself.

The newly completed third floor of the west wing of the hospital housed the cardiac unit. The modern four bed renovation was the construction beneficiary of one of Fedderson's foundation connections. An additional $40,000 was provided to supply area churches, schools, and libraries with AEDs, those ubiquitous portable emergency heart defibrillator machines that support life and cardiac issues, and, of course onsite emergency training. It was true: foundation money followed Fedderson. The money was given anonymously-without memorializing the grantor. It seemed out of place to many not to have a plaque adorn the wall of such a generous gift. But as Fedderson put it, "Never disagree with the terms of a great deal when it cost you nothing."

The unit was intended to respond to local cardiac emergencies while the patient was waiting transfer to the larger and more experienced Geisinger Hospital System in Scranton or a quick flight to Philadelphia or Penn State-Hershey. Nonetheless, it was state of the art. The newly named unit's medical director was a close friend of Joan Evans and her husband, Alan, Dr. Laura Rankin.

The phone call from the hospital cardiac unit awakened Rankin from a deep sleep. Astonished that the patient was Evans, she hastily dressed and drove the four miles to the hospital. The emergency room staff had quickly assembled the medical data needed to assess and diagnose the arterial blockages and recommended immediate surgery. Rankin concurred and performed the triple bypass surgery that saved her friend's life. Several hours later, Evans rested in one of the new Hill-Rom surgical beds in the cardiac care unit. Because of the severity of the surgical procedure, every patient in that unit was considered "critical." A myriad of technology connected medicines and electronics with IV bags that fed and pumped a cocktail of rejuvenation into Evans. Prayer and science encouraged a full recovery.

Immediately outside the unit, the "Family and Visitors" waiting room was filling to overflow capacity. Alan was busy telling and re-telling the events that led up to his finding Joan on the floor. The common responses were shock, disbelief, and personal self-reflection that ended with the oft acknowledged consensus: heart attacks can happen to anyone, even me.

The hospital staff was in a state of disbelief about Dr. Evans's heart attack. "She's so young and healthy looking," was the topic sentence of the conversation. The executive director of the Women's Wellness Clinic where she volunteered issued a statement calling for "well wishes and positive thoughts for such a courageous leader of women's reproductive rights."

By mid-afternoon in another part of town, TV crews and live "on location" news outlets had located and collared Steve Williams, the baby's father, who seemed genuinely saddened by the news of the death of his child, even wiping a tear from his eye at the end of the interview. He even surprised Armstadt with his emotional response to the event.

Frederick Nichols had taken refuge in Fedderson's office to avoid the press and to watch the televised proceedings. "You're really upset this time you bastard," blurted Doug Fedderson aloud to the crying image of Steve Williams on the TV in his office. "You're upset because the gravy train pulled out of the station and left you behind," he added sarcastically.

Nichols looked at Fedderson. "Well Doug, my end is covered. The child's transfer occurred quickly and without any external complications. I'll be in touch with Grayson later today. The Care Team has their instructions and the plans haven't changed."

"Now we wait," he replied. "Will you be leaving?"

"I think so," Nichols said as he sipped coffee. "I think so."

"It's hard I know," Fedderson added.

"I was hoping we could avoid this," he sighed. "By the way have you spoken with Joan's family? Have you spoken with Alan?" Nichols asked.

"Vivian called me last night," said Fedderson. "She heard the news from some of her police friends. After the whole thing went viral the whole damn hospital decided to call me. I met Alan at the hospital after the surgery. He was shaken but relieved and hopeful about the outcome."

"My prayers are with Joan and her family," Nichols added.

"Fred, you're the doctor of record for Baby Franco. Once the press learn of your offer to pay for funeral expenses you'll become walking human-interest story. They'll want to talk with you, know about your reasons for stepping forward like you did, and most importantly, did you realize she would die so soon."

"What do you suggest?"

"The press is unavoidable in this case, but manageable," said Fedderson. "It's just a matter of learning the tactic of cooperative avoidance."

"What are you talking about?"

"Recall that boring and innocuous are buzz words on how to react to the press. You want as little to do with the press as possible, but you don't want to piss them off or pique their curiosity."

"Ideally, I want them to leave me alone."

"Exactly. Now here's how to do that. Begin by being very cooperative with them. Polite, cooperative, and very, very long-winded."

"Long-winded?"

"Right, bore the hell out of them, lots of medical jargon, a few Latin phrases and the like and eventually they'll leave you alone. All they want is a sound bite. Verbose and boring doesn't easily fit into a TV or radio sound bite. And every three or four words put your hand to your mouth, and clear your throat and say, 'excuse me.' That'll make you a real pain in the ass to edit."

"So, cooperate but be boring and verbose," said Dr. Nichols understanding Fedderson's example.

"For now channel a dull congressman or how about, er, what's his name…the Chairman of the Federal Reserve some years ago. You might remember him. The man's a genius, and not so much for his economic policies. But did you ever hear him speak? He's duller than a high school freshman reading Cicero. He talks that economics jargon no one understands. He was in office for years and in all that time he's got one sound bite to his credit – years ago he described the forces behind the bullish stock market as 'irrational exuberance.' He wanted the stock market to cool off and that two-word phrase did it. Uses the media for his own purposes. Man's a genius."

"OK, I'll adopt the 'dull is good' theory in all my dealings with the press," said Nichols. Fedderson's phone rang. The hospital administrator picked up the receiver.

"He was? What'd he want? Yeah," he covered the mouthpiece and whispered to Nichols, "Williams is downstairs," he said.

"The father?" asked Dr. Nichols. "What's he want?"

"Wait," said Fedderson to Nichols, and then uncovering the mouthpiece asked, "So where is he now? No. No, that's fine. Thanks for telling me." He hung up the phone.

"That was Security," continued Fedderson. "Apparently Williams has been drinking and wanted to see his daughter. The guard told him the body isn't here and Williams says he wants to see a cop, the guard says he's a cop and Williams then asked for a reporter. So the guard walked him outside and Williams hooks up with some newspaperwoman. She offered to take him to the funeral home. A heart-wrenching exclusive in the making, no doubt. Well, at least he isn't making trouble here."

"Someone should call Grayson," said Nichols, "let him know the bum's on his way. If he's been drinking, there may be trouble there."

"I'll call him. Where can I reach you if I need to?"

"I'll be in my office until 2."

"Now, remember, don't say anything controversial about baby Franco and take a long time to say it and keep clearing your throat."

Meanwhile the town of 4,300 was awash with media. Reporters gathered in and around both the hospital the Grayson Funeral Home. The large Victorian house made a great backdrop for newscasters televising "live on the scene" to report on the death of Baby Franco. Evans' heart attack would forever be only a footnote.

After Nichols left, Fedderson called Grayson to warn him that Williams going to the funeral home. But Williams did not go to the funeral home immediately. Instead he conned the reporter into buying him lunch at a bar near the funeral home.

****

Williams's lunch with the reporter from the *Times* was preceded and followed by several beers. After an hour, the reporter, realizing that William only reminded her of her last boring and drunken boyfriend correctly surmised the interview was going nowhere, paid her share of the bill and left the bar. Williams stayed and allowed other sympathetic patrons to buy him drinks until near closing time.

He left the bar around 2 a.m. drunk and, determined to go to the funeral home, slowly traversed the several blocks to Grayson's. He rounded the corner of White and Rail Street, stopped and stared at the Victorian building that housed the funeral home. "My baby," he mumbled, "Cold and alone. What kind of father am I?" he questioned his character as he steeled himself to what he believed he had to do. He had to be with his daughter, now and at all costs. A full moon shone on the street. He hesitated and stumbled along. He steadied himself as he haltingly walked following the retaining wall feeling his way to the banister at the bottom of the steps. He smiled as he ascended the stone walkway that led to the expansive wrap around porch. "What the hell am I doing here," he thought to himself. "This place is closed! Shit!" He looked around at the empty night and felt out of place. "Oh well, I'm here." He broke a window on the side of the Victorian house porch, and squeezed through and entered the purple carpeted hallway separating the richly appointed viewing rooms. The first room was empty.

"Where is she?" he said aloud.

The viewing room across the hall was also empty and

he made his way down the hall to a set of stairs to the basement. "Maybe, here." Fumbling and bumbling he stumbled into the embalming room in the basement. He noticed the small white coffin in the corner. He solemnly approached it.

Avery Grayson, having been awakened by the sound of the window breaking and Williams stumbling around, had called the police and was now slowly making his way from his living quarters on the third floor to investigate.

He found Williams in the embalming room, and, recognizing him as the father of the infant, he turned on the light, causing Williams to literally jump with fright.

"Shit," said Grayson, "How'd you get in here?"

"My baby..." said Williams.

"Never mind that," said Grayson, "everything will be alright. Here, let me help you upstairs. We've got to hurry; the cops are on the way..."

"Cops," said Williams. "Good. Bring 'em on. I want to see the cops."

When the two men arrived upstairs, Grayson sat Williams in the empty viewing room and dialed 911 from the extension phone in the hallway.

When the dispatcher answered Grayson spoke hurriedly, "This is Avery Grayson at the Grayson Funeral..."

"Yes, sir, we've logged your earlier call. A patrol car is on the way."

"Well, that's why I called. It's a false alarm, you can call them back... everything is... well, never mind."

Grayson slowly put the receiver down as headlights from the responding patrol car swept across the room.

Grayson went to the front door, opened it and stepped out onto the porch. He slowly closed the door behind him, and turned to greet the officers who were climbing the stairs.

"Avery, is that you?" said the officer closest to Grayson. "It's me, Curt."

"Hey, Curt, sorry about this," said Grayson.

"Everything is fine, false alarm. I tried to call back but you guys got here so quick."

"You sure? We could have a look around," said Curt.

"No, no need. I just got spooked by a picture that fell from the wall. Broken glass, lots of noise. Woke me up out of a sound sleep and I called 911. I'm still half asleep."

Williams then threw open the front door and stumbled onto the porch. "Ah, the police, good. Help me find my baby."

"OK, Avery, who's that?" said Curt.

"Look Curt, I didn't want any trouble. That's the father of the little girl who died, the one that's been so sick."

"Oh, yeah, it is him," said Curt's partner.

"Damn right it's me and I want to see my baby. My baby. I've got rights."

"Yes, Mr. Williams," said Grayson. "I'll be right with you. Just let me explain to the officers here. Anyway, this guy has had a rough day, the worst. You can see he's pretty tanked up. Well, he came over, broke in, and he wants to see his kid. I'm not going to press charges against him. Who would, after what he's been through? So, I'll take him inside, give him a private viewing and he'll leave quietly."

"That's fine, Avery," said Curt, "but I don't think it's a good idea to leave you here alone with this bird. In his state you can't tell how he'll react. Why don't we wait till you show him the baby, then we can take him on home. He can't drive or walk home in this condition."

"Well, gee. That's fine. Just fine. OK, guys, come on in," Grayson continued leading the three men from the porch to the foyer. "I'll take Mr. Williams to the baby and then he'll be ready to go. Tell you what. I've got a few things that need to be done first, you know to get ready. If you could, hold Mr. Williams here. I'll bring the deceased into the viewing room on the right side of the hall. There's an elevator. So I won't need any help. Only take a minute, I appreciate your willingness to help out."

Grayson disappeared down the stairs.

"How you doing, fella?" said Curt to Williams.

"Where's my baby?" said Williams. "I looked. Can't find no baby."

"Yeah, well, Avery will have the baby here for you in a few minutes. You'll have a few minutes alone with her, but then we've got to go."

"You can't arrest me, I've got rights. I want to see my baby."

"You will. You will. Take it easy. We're not arresting you. We're here to help," said the second officer as the elevator brought the white coffin to a room on the second floor behind the viewing rooms. Several minutes later Avery Grayson appeared in the hallway.

"I'll just take him in, for a few minutes," said Avery. "If you could wait here, he'd probably like to have this be as private as possible under the circumstances. I'll just dim the lights for privacy, you understand."

"Sure, Avery, we'll stay right here," said Curt. "OK, buddy, Mr. Grayson will take you to see the baby now."

"I've got rights," said Williams, "rights."

"Yes, you do," said Grayson. "Here, we'll just go into this room, and you can see the baby."

The two officers waited in the hallway until they heard Williams yell, "This is no goddamn' baby!" followed by Grayson's plea, "Mr. Williams, please, put her down, don't."

And then there was a crash.

"Jesus," said both officers in unison as they ran to the door.

"Not a shittin' baby," slurred Williams, pointing to the small figure that had landed on the carpeted floor about eight feet from the empty coffin. "Not a baby, goddam fake!"

Grayson sat in the first row of chairs for mourners, hands cradling his lowered head. When the officers ran into the room, Grayson jumped to his feet saying, "I'll take care of it. Just leave her there, and get this guy out of here."

Williams pushed the coffin, which was on a wheeled

84

gurney, out of his way and grabbed Grayson as the funeral director attempted to move to the lifeless form on the floor.

Officer Curt Foley ran to Grayson's aid as Williams continued to scream, "Where's the baby, you son of a bitch, where's the baby?"

"Calm down, sir, just calm down," said Curt, "I don't want to place you under arrest…"

"Arrest him, he's got the baby and he won't show me, it's my baby."

"Sir," said Curt, "the baby was in the coffin."

"A shittin' fake, a fake…"

"No, the baby is dead, they don't look real with the makeup and all," said Curt.

"Jesus, Curt," said the second officer. "He's right."

"What?" said Curt, turning to his partner.

"It's a doll," said the officer. "This is a doll," said the officer, holding out the life-size, toy baby doll.

"Avery," said Curt, "what's going on? Where's the baby? The father wants to see the baby."

"I want an attorney," said Grayson.

CHAPTER 7

The insistent ringing urged Dan Hewitt from a deep sleep. Head in his pillow, he extended his right hand toward the clock radio and made several ineffective slaps in the general vicinity of the snooze button. The ringing continued. He turned, sat up and stared uncomprehendingly at the clock radio for a moment before awaking enough to realize what was happening.

"Phone," he mumbled aloud to himself while reaching for the phone that shared the nightstand with the clock radio and several books in progress.

"Hewitt," he rasped while trying to stretch himself awake.

"Sorry to wake you, Sarge."

"S'OK, I had to get up to answer the phone anyway."

"Yeah, right, good one. This is Granger on the night desk. Sorry to bother you…"

"Has something happened?"

"Yes and No. I'm calling about, well, it's this weird incident..."

"Weird...?"

"Missing body, from Grayson's Funeral Home."

"Someone copped a corpse?"

"Well, the body's missing. It's that Baby Franco kid..."

"The one that's been in the news, mother was in a car accident?"

"That's the one."

"The baby's body is missing?"

"They can't find it. The father showed up about an hour ago at Grayson's and attempted to conduct a private wake after hours..."

"He did what?"

"Looks like he broke into the funeral home to see the kid and the body wasn't there."

"What's Grayson say?"

"Won't talk, he wants his lawyer."

"I'm on my way," said Hewitt hanging up the phone. "The glamour of police work," he muttered aloud as he climbed back into the clothes he has tossed on the floor the previous evening. He dressed quickly and noticed that it was 3:45 a.m. "Damn it. Somebody somewhere owes me a good night's sleep."

When he arrived at Grayson's Funeral Home he found two police officers trying to calm an obviously intoxicated Steve Williams. Grayson was sitting on a chair near the office door, head in his hands. Hewitt nodded to the officers on duty.

"Foley, Brill, what do we have here?" Officer Foley left Steve Williams with Officer Brill and walked to Hewitt to conduct a semi-private hallway conference summarizing the recent events.

"Thanks for coming so soon, Detective," said Foley. "Here's what we got. Officer Brill and I responded to Mr. Grayson's 911 call about a break-in at the funeral home. We found Mr. Williams here causing a disturbance and, understanding his situation, tried to calm him down. He wanted to see his daughter, the coma-mom's baby, the car accident, you know the one."

Detective Hewitt nodded.

"Right," continued Foley. "Anyway, Mr. Grayson tried to calm the guy down. Took him into one of the viewing rooms. And that's when all hell broke loose. Williams insisted on opening the coffin, and he went ballistic when he realized his daughter wasn't inside the coffin, just a doll."

"A doll?"

"Yeah, a big one, the kind that cries, 'Mama'."

"Did Grayson explain how the doll got there?"

"He won't talk, says he wants an attorney. That's when we stopped talking to him and asked for you."

Glancing at his watch, Hewitt asked, "What did you do about the attorney?"

"We just said we understood that he wanted to call his attorney," said Brill.

"You didn't stop him from calling, you didn't tell him he couldn't call..."

"Nope"

"But he hasn't called?"

"Not yet, Detective. We haven't said or done anything to stop him, but it isn't our job to dial the number for him."

"OK. Has anyone looked for the body?"

"Officer Brill walked through the house. Grayson gave him permission. And he looked around outside, too. Nothing. I stayed with Avery and the father."

"OK, take a few more officers and do another search outside. Check garbage cans, sewer drains, and don't scare the neighbors," said Hewitt. "Stay out of front and back yards. Just search along the street in both directions."

When Foley left, Hewitt turned his attention to Avery Grayson seated some 20 feet away from him, head still in his hands, staring at the floor. He walked right up to Grayson's side. Grayson didn't budge.

"Avery..." said Detective Hewitt.

No reaction.

"Avery... it's me, Dan Hewitt."

Grayson slowly looked up at the detective.

"Oh, hi Dan."

"Avery," said Hewitt, "can you help us out here? Any idea where the body is?"

"I've asked for an attorney. I'm not talking to anyone until I talk to an attorney."

"Jesus, Avery, no one has accused you of anything.

Not even sure a crime has been committed. I mean we're talking about a dead body here. Might be some minor health code violation. But when a guy asks for an attorney, well it just naturally makes me suspicious."

"A suspicious detective. There's news. I was the last person known to have a corpse that has turned up missing. I've got a raving drunk father accusing me of God knows what, a house full of cops and I'm supposed to leave myself unprotected and forego the advice of an attorney just so I don't raise the suspicions of a detective who is called out to investigate a non-crime at 4 a.m. in the morning. I'm not saying another word until I speak to my attorney."

As Grayson was speaking, Officer Brill did not notice that Williams had risen slowly until the still drunken father made a leap for the funeral director.

"Where's my kid, my baby girl," Williams shouted as he lunged toward Grayson, pushing Hewitt aside. "What did you do with her, you damn pervert!" He reached for Grayson's neck, screaming, "I'll kill you, you sicko!"

Hewitt and Brill pried Williams from Grayson.

"Get him the hell out of here," said Hewitt. "Put him in the patrol car. If he gives you any more trouble, lock him up on a drunk and disorderly."

"Me, you're gonna lock me up, he's the one..." argued Williams as Officer Brill led him from the room.

"Williams," said Brill sternly, "the best thing for you to do right now is to keep your mouth shut. Don't make me arrest you. The local jail is not the best place to nurse a hangover the size of the one you're going to have."

Brill was able to urge Williams outside and into the patrol car.

"OK, Avery," said Hewitt after Foley had taken Williams to the car. "It's just me and you. I know this has been rough on you. But help me out. How'd the doll get in the coffin? Is the doll something used in packing? Like a demo..."

89

"No." Avery paused for several seconds. "I put the doll in the coffin."

"Why?"

"The guy broke in. He was drunk. You saw him. He wanted to see the baby. The body was gone. I wasn't about to try to reason with him. You saw him."

"Where was the last place you saw the body?"

Grayson paused before answering wearily, "In the embalming room, downstairs. But it wasn't there. I was still groggy from sleep, scared. I panicked. Officers Foley and Brill were here, I've known Curt Foley all my life. I was going to tell him about the missing body, but not in front of the father, not in his condition. So I tried to trick Williams. I put the doll in the coffin. Christ, those damn things look so real. Who would have thought that drunken bastard would pick it up."

"So where'd you get the doll?"

"We've got some toys here. Kids get restless, we've got a few toys in a room back there," said Grayson, pointing to a side room in the hallway. I went back there, grabbed a doll and put it in the coffin. Honest to God, I never thought he'd notice. Once he was gone, I was going to report the missing body."

"OK, now that's a help. Appreciate it. So when was the last time you saw the body?"

"Look," said Grayson, "I must insist that you let me call my lawyer. I've said more than I wanted to say. I want to cooperate, but I've got a huge mess on my hands here."

"Avery," said Hewitt, "It's your place, you're not under arrest, make the call." Hewitt glanced at his watch. "Although it is just after 4 in the morning, dial the number. But, I'll bet you'll be getting him up a bit earlier than he'd like."

"I don't care," said Grayson. "I need legal advice. There are civil issues. This is a place of business. I could lose everything. When word gets out that a body was stolen from my funeral home, oh, man--people expect dead bodies to stay put. People won't leave their dead pets in the hands of a funeral director that loses bodies. This could ruin me. Could lose my license. We're talking about my whole life here. I've got to make that call. Excuse me."

Grayson walked to his office and picked up the phone and dialed the home number of Ralph Fitzmorris, waking the attorney from a deep sleep.

Hewitt prowled the hallway deep in thought. Officer Foley returned to report on the brief search of the neighborhood.

"OK, Detective," said Foley. "We've got four men searching around the house and along the sidewalks up and down the street. In a couple of hours we can use dog teams to search the surrounding yards without alarming the neighbors."

"Good, that's fine. Listen, Dave," said Hewitt, "Give me a play-by-play of when you first got here."

"We got a call that there had been a break in, we pulled up, Curt got out of the car first. He was on the steps of the porch when Grayson popped out of the front door saying there had been a false alarm."

"He said that?"

"Yeah, he wanted us to go. Then Williams jumps out onto the porch ranting about the missing baby. We try to calm the guy down. Grayson offered to set up a private viewing hoping that would satisfy the guy. Grayson told us he didn't want to press charges for the break in, you know, because of what the father had been through and all."

"But initially, Grayson wanted you to leave."

"Yep. Must have thought he could handle Williams on his own. But I don't see how. I mean Williams was out of control. And Grayson isn't that strong a guy. So anyway, Curt and I give the father a few minutes alone in the viewing room; we just stayed in the hallway just outside the room until we hear screaming and stuff being thrown around the room. Curt and I run in, I go over to what I think is the corpse on the floor and Dave goes to peel Williams off Grayson and that's when I picked up the doll."

"Then what?"

"Grayson asks for his lawyer here and we ask for you. That's it."

"What do you make of it, Foley?"

"Gives me the creeps."

"Yeah," said Hewitt, "But the body--did the father take it when he broke in and, who knows, lose it in the house or outside somewhere? Or did Grayson, I don't know, what the hell can you do with a corpse--sell it? Who to and for what? Organs? Tissue? Stem cell experiments?"

"Man, this is getting creepier. Maybe it's a cult."

"A cult, what kind of cult?"

"I don't know. A cult. A worshiping a dead baby cult. Or maybe it was a prank."

"Some prank," said Hewitt.

"Plenty of nuts out there. Remember the incident when those two kids wanted to know what it was like to kill someone so they ordered a pizza for delivery way the hell out at some abandoned farm. Delivery kid shows up and these two slackers whack him. Crazy nuts don't need a reason for doing anything. That's what makes them nuts."

"What's your take on this, detective?"

"My instincts tell me Grayson knows more than he is saying. With the father, I get the feeling he says more than he knows. And, after 18 years as a cop, I can tell you one thing about my instincts."

"What's that?"

"Sometimes they're right, and sometimes they're wrong. What the hell, they're only instincts," said Hewitt smiling.

Hewitt's instincts were fully alert now and he was anything but comfortable with Grayson's story. If Grayson intended to tell officers Foley or Brill about the missing body, why did he try to get them to leave? If he did get the cops to leave he may have thought he could fool the drunken father. There would be a closed coffin funeral and no one would find out about the missing body. But why?

Hewitt phoned his boss, Joe Wallington, Chief of Honesdale Police. Chief Wallington then phoned the county prosecutor, Henry Silva. Two hours later the trio was meeting at a coffee shop near the funeral home to discuss the situation.

"So, Dan," said Silva, "busy night for you guys-one missing body, one drunken father, one funeral director wanting his attorney to counsel him. What do you plan for tonight's excitement? You really should do something about the crime rate in this town."

"Well, Henry, if you prosecutors would give up that plea bargaining crap and put some of these creeps away, we might not be dealing with this crime crazy environment and the streets might be safe for the good citizens of our community."

"Actually, the streets seem to be OK, we need to beef up security in the embalming rooms and funeral parlors of this fair town," said Hewitt.

"Yeah, it's been a weird night," said Wallington. "What do you think, Dan?"

"We're going to trace the path of the baby. We'll start at the hospital; talk with doctors, nurses, anyone who might have had contact with the little one. Even visitors to the hospital, nursery…a lot of routine police leg work. And we'll follow any lead."

"What, you think there's some connection with the missing body as far back as the hospital?" wondered Wallington.

"We think there's a connection somewhere," pointed out Hewitt, "Our missing baby was delivered and treated at the hospital. It has to start there."

"Good thinking," said Wallington, "99 times out of a

hundred, what's obvious turns out to be what's true. But then, on the other hand, coincidence ain't connection. We're dealing with a sick-o. That's for sure. And remember; don't let the weird distract you from the obvious, Dan."

"That's good advice, Chief," said Hewitt, "99 times out of 100."

"Play those odds every day, my boy, and you have a stellar career in police work ahead of you," the chief promised.

"I'm with the Chief on his one," offered Silva. "Focus your energy on this missing dead baby thing. Find the connections. What does your gut tell you?" asked Silva.

"I don't know what to think," said Hewitt. "Grayson has been a respected businessman in the community for years. Family business, second generation. He says he picked up the body of the child from the hospital morgue early yesterday morning and did not realize it was missing until Williams breaking in awakened him. He admits putting the doll in the coffin, but only as a ruse to try and calm the hysterical father."

"There was a quick search of the funeral home," said Chief of Police Wallington.

"That's right, Joe," said Hewitt. "They searched the premises and found nothing. Frankly, if the body was anywhere in the house and Grayson knew about it, we have to assume he would simply have put it in the coffin for the father."

"If it was all in one piece," said Wallington.

"Thank you for that image, Chief," said Silva, "I didn't want this Danish anyway," he replied pushing the strawberry filled croissant to the side.

"Why you guys with weak stomachs insist on getting involved in police work gets me. You'd have to go a long way to find another job where you get paid to look hard and long at so many nasty things."

"Like sitting across from you at breakfast?"

"So why does he cut up the body if indeed he did?" asked Hewitt.

"I don't know. They say they use fetal tissue for treatment of Alzheimer's..."

"This isn't a fetus, it's an infant, nearly two months old, too old for that stem cell stuff, I imagine," said Hewitt.

"Not much damn difference as far as I can see," said the Chief. "What the hell, he might have been making sausage. Sort of reminds me of ..."

"Yeah, yeah," interrupted Hewitt.

"You want me to come up with a logical reason for someone cutting up an infant corpse?"

"Henry," said Hewitt, "can we get a search warrant for Grayson's Funeral Home?"

"And the grounds for the search warrant would be..?"

"He says the baby was there. Now it's gone. It's a crime scene, but it is also his place of business. He won't voluntarily let us search the place again, certainly his attorney won't. I think Grayson's dirty. If he weren't, he'd be more cooperative, I know it. It's my gut feeling."

"I can't get a search warrant just because you have a gut feeling about the guy, that you think he's dirty," said Silva. "Hell, that gut feeling could be the result of those four sausages you've eaten so far."

"It's a crime scene, he's my primary suspect," said Hewitt. "He was the last one to see the corpse, he lied to the police when they first arrived, tried to get them to leave and he told me he had every intention of reporting the missing body to one of those police. If we get a search warrant and pull a lot of stuff out of there, business records and all, we'll make Grayson sweat."

"You say it's a crime scene," said Silva. "What's the crime?"

"Depends what was done with the body," said Hewitt, "but at the very least we could charge him with providing false and misleading information to the police."

95

"How am I going to get a judge to go along with issuing a search warrant on such a flimsy charge?" asked Silva.

"Weave that interpersonal magic of yours. Charm him. Tell him it's an ongoing investigation. We don't know what this will lead to, a stolen body ring, some crazy cult, witches coven, we need the search warrant," argued Hewitt.

"You know, Henry," said Chief Wallington confidently, "if you brought the request to Judge Collins..."

"As an ex-prosecutor, Judge Collins at times gives us some leeway on search warrants. But we're not giving him much to work with. These are weak grounds," said Silva.

"He'd throw any one of the assistant prosecutors right out of the room," said the chief. "But if you bring the request to him, he'll recognize that you need a little help with this one and he'll give it to you. You know he will. And when you're a judge, you'll do the same when the county prosecutor comes to you for help, provided you're of the same political persuasion. So you see your vote does count."

You know what they say, 'Good attorneys know the law; great ones know the judge,'" said Silva.

Ralph Fitzmorris, Grayson's attorney, entered the coffee shop and paused in the doorway, searching the room. Once he saw the chief, Silva, and Hewitt, he walked directly to their booth.

"Penny for your thoughts, gentlemen."

"How are you, Ralph? Nasty business, eh?" said Silva. "How's Avery doing?"

"Devastated. These unfortunate events have the potential to destroy his livelihood," said Fitzmorris, "even though he had nothing to do with the disappearance of the body."

"Sounds like you're on the job, Ralph. You taking the case?" asked Hewitt.

"I'm not aware of any case to take at this point, unless you gentlemen have some information you'd like to share with me." He paused momentarily. "No? Good. However, as Mr. Grayson's attorney for better than 15 years, I will continue to represent him during this unpleasantness. Let me get to the point. Henry, will you be filing charges against my client?"

"The investigation is continuing, Ralph. And we would like to have your client's cooperation."

"You have and will continue to have his full cooperation under the law. But if there are no charges being brought at this time, we respectfully request that you get the police out of his house and off his property. He's got a wake to prepare for."

"A terrible case," said Wallington, "breaks your heart. It really does. But tell me, Ralph. How do you conduct a wake when there isn't a body to bury? As an attorney might you consider the literal Latin translation of *habeas corpus* at this time? It means 'we have the body'."

"Always the comic, Joe," he replied. "So what do you say," said Fitzmorris, "can you please call off your men?"

"Chief," said Silva, "have your men pull out."

"Will do. I'll meet you at the car. Remember, I'm your ride back to the office," said the chief, excusing himself from the booth.

"Thank you, Henry, and you too, Chief," said Fitzmorris. "Tell me, are you investigating Mr. Williams? He admits breaking into my client's home and place of business and we believe he removed the body."

"There is only so much we can do. Your client refuses to press charges against the father for the break-in. Any idea why the father would take the body?"

"Who can say what the combination of grief and alcohol will do to a man," said Fitzmorris.

"Well, Ralph," said Silva, "someone is responsible for the disappearance of that body. The father is one possibility, and your client is another. After that we're

97

looking for person or persons unknown to us at this time. We haven't completely discounted the father's involvement in this."

"And why would you, when, after all, the investigation is continuing," said Fitzmorris. "I appreciate your time and candor, and now if you'll excuse me."

"Certainly Ralph, we'll be talking," said Silva.

Henry Silva left the coffee shop shortly after Fitzmorris. He stopped to speak with Chief Wallington, who was at his car.

"Chief, this is going to be a real circus with the press and all. I'm going to call on Judge Collins. I want more than a search warrant. I'm going to ask him to seal the hospital records on the baby girl. Also, let's get a list of all hospital personnel involved in the baby's care--the works as Dan suggested. If I ask for the world now, he'll believe we're onto something hot."

News of the missing body swept through the town. Residents lined up on various sides of the 'who-stole-the-body' controversy, with the father garnering a goodly share of votes as body snatcher and bona fide cult member. Williams, as an outsider prone to public drunkenness and maudlin pleas in front of TV cameras, was an easy target of suspicion. Avery Grayson was the hometown boy. But as an undertaker he generated suspicion in the minds of some residents, who, if they thought about undertakers at all, felt uneasy about anyone engaged in such an unpleasant business. These prejudiced souls could readily accept the notion that Grayson routinely supplied bodies for use in medical experiments, as did, they were sure, all undertakers.

Another popular rumor involved a witches' coven, and there were the obligatory conspiracy mavens who blamed the government for everything and were certain that the body had been stolen by the CIA to hide the fact that the child was the president's illegitimate issue. There were some crazy rumors, too.

****

Later that morning Noreen Ryan, Fedderson's assistant, was meeting with the staff of the trauma unit and intensive care unit of the hospital. The topic of conversation centered on the recovery of Janice Franco. Plans for her being air-lifted to Scranton for intensive intervention were scrapped after EEG readings and other monitored data showed improvement. Her breathing and other bodily functions improved to the point that she was experiencing periods of alertness and talkativeness. Although sedated, those medications were being reduced. Eventually the topic of her child and the mess surrounding the father surfaced.

"Yes, thank you for bringing up the elephant in the room," Ryan stated. "But let's keep perspective. I consider discussing that specific question pure gossip until all the facts are clear. Defer any questions to Dr. Nichols, the baby's pediatrician. The baby died this morning and is at the Grayson Funeral Home. That's all we have to know at this time."

****

By lunchtime attorney Sidney Armstadt and his client Steve Williams were back on TV.

Williams was able to repeat for the benefit of cameras and microphone the following tearful litany, "All I can say is that I want to see my baby laid to rest. These past two days have been a living hell for me. This just ain't right. It's sick. But I'm not out for revenge. I just want them to return the body."

Williams again blubbered his heartfelt anguish into the bank of microphones in the parking lot across the street from Grayson's Funeral Home.

"Steve, thank you, this is difficult, we know. Difficult. Very hard for you," said Armstadt, as he gently

99

moved his client aside and assumed the position in front of the cameras and microphones. He adjusted his tie.

"It is evident, quite evident, perfectly clear, the extent of mental anguish, the torture and mental pain and suffering that my client has undergone and continues to go through as a result of this unspeakable, this unholy, uncivilized incident. We want to thank the police and county prosecutor's office for all their efforts to solve this heinous crime. Just heinous. We are pleased, very happy with their efforts and with the direction the investigation is going."

"Is Mr. Williams a suspect?" asked one reporter.

"If he were," said Armstadt, "do you think I would be pleased with the investigation? I don't think so, not at all. No. Not at all. Nothing pleasing in that. Nothing. My client has assisted the police wherever and however he could in this investigation. We are confident they will soon break this case."

An unintelligible tangle of shouted questions rose up from the reporters as Armstadt waved goodbye and walked his client, arm in arm, out of camera range.

"How's that, Sid?" Williams asked.

"Effective, quite effective. Very good. But we've got to keep you under wraps for a while. Stay out of the public eye, can't overdo it, mustn't overdo it. And stay sober. Must be careful. Stay on our toes, Steve, on our toes. It's cerebral, a head game. Mental anguish. The pain has to be believable. Terrible pain. Must be real. Must be sympathetic. Get them with you. Have them on your side. Get them to dislike your well-insured opponent and like you. That's the key to convincing a jury to be generous, very generous, with someone else's money. Magnanimous."

****

Chief Joe Wallington turned off the TV, causing the doughy face of Armstadt to quickly fade to black.

"Damn it, Hewitt," said the chief, "I just hate to see that lawyer and that creep father benefit from any of this."

"A couple of snakes to be sure, Chief," said Hewitt. "I've got sources at the hospital that tell me he practically requested a payoff in return for discontinuing treatment for the child."

"A fine human being," said the chief. "I was wondering what their game was. Can you think of any reason why Williams or Armstadt would want the body removed?"

"The only thing that motivates those two is money. I don't see how they'd make any money off the disappearance of the body, except a lawsuit against the funeral home. That's a long way to go to work a settlement with an insurance company. I don't think they're involved. They're just hanging around the edges looking for an opportunity to cash in on whatever develops. The hospital tells me that the infant's body and tissues were practically worthless for research or transplants because of her medical condition, the level and type of medications in her bloodstream."

"Well, somebody took the body. And presumably they had a reason to do so, wouldn't you think? But if not Grayson or Williams, who?" said the chief.

"Chief," said Hewitt, "we're at the front end of this thing. We've got to put a little more pressure on Grayson, I'm sure he's the key. But while we wait for the search warrant, let's take a step back and look at the hospital. Check their procedures in handling death cases and the like. I want to review what actually transpired in the final hours of the child at the hospital. Who released the child to Grayson? Who called the medical examiner? Someone had to record the death and give permission to release the body."

****

Philip Duran glanced at his watch as he entered the National Bank Center and headed for his suite on the 23rd floor. He walked into his office and was greeted by his secretary, Dorothy Ellis. He was returning from a brunch at Old Original Bookbinder's. A local CPA firm was sponsoring a "meet and greet" and he seldom missed any opportunity to expand his business especially when someone else was paying the bill.

"Isn't it dreadful, Mr. Duran, the way they treated that dead child and her father..."

"Who? I'm sorry; I haven't been listening to the news. What happened," he asked offhandedly.

"It's all over the news…the one up in Honesdale, the baby with the mother in a coma. Baby Franco. Her body is missing. Someone stole the child's corpse and placed a doll in the coffin. The police are investigating. It's such a shame."

Duran looked stunned, "My God."

"I feel the same way. You just don't know what this world is coming to," she replied.

His tenor changed. "Dorothy, tell you what. It's not fair that I've been out all day on this gorgeous day and you've been cramped up here. Why don't you take lunch now and spend the rest of the day in the park, or call your husband and surprise him with dinner tonight on me. I just want you to know I appreciate all you do."

"Are you kidding?" she said with a smile. "Because if you are, I'm going to get really annoyed at you. But if you're not, I'll see to it that you go to Bookbinder's for lunch more often."

Forcing a laugh, Duran said, "Great! So be it. Go and enjoy your day. All deadlines are extended another day!"

He smiled as she hastily grabbed her coat and left the office.

He locked his office door and glanced at the second cell phone on his belt clip. The message blinked - *One missed call*, three hours ago. No message. "Dammit," he murmured, "Got to remember to keep the burner phone activated. He wondered why there wasn't a second call or a message. Alarmed, he went directly to the cabinet at the end of the far wall. Opening the top draw, he retrieved several bulky files and carefully fed the contents into the paper shredder next to his desk.

****

Later that afternoon despite the warm March weather, Dr. Fred Nichols was preparing to start a fire in his fireplace. He placed two Duraflame logs on the metal grates in the hearth. He placed several stacks of patient files on top of the logs and stuck several quick-igniting fire sticks between the pages. He struck a match. "That should do it," he said as the flames burned out of control consuming the pages of medical records.

CHAPTER 8

The next day Hewitt arrived at the three story brick and stone police station just before 7 a.m. The Main street building was home to 14 officers and displayed a faded "Mail Pouch Tobacco" sign on the side of the building. The sign and the country culture reminded the townsfolk of the 'good old days' when Horatio Allen fired up the "Stourbridge Lion", the first commercial locomotive in the United States. Originally known as Dyberry Forks, the town changed its name to Honesdale to honor Philip Hone, first president of the D&H Canal Company, a coal transport company that carried coal to New York City in the 1830's. To locals, the lakeland area offers a quiet way of life, more rural than suburban.

Hewitt completed his police training in Morris County, NJ and was hired as a patrolman for the Morristown PD that same year. His years on the force were seldom enlivened by major crimes. The only time he unholstered his standard issue handgun was to clean it.

He was a bit player in the Sidney J. Reso kidnap and murder case. Reso, the 57-year-old president of a large multi-national company, said goodbye to his wife one morning and left for work. His car never made it past the end of the 250-foot driveway of his home. Wounded during the abduction, Reso was locked in a wooden box and placed in a commercial storage unit, where he died following four days without food or water. The kidnappers dumped his body in a shallow grave in the New Jersey Pine Barrens.

Hewitt was part of the amalgamated FBI arrest team that apprehended a former company security guard and his wife for kidnapping the executive. The couple later pled guilty to kidnapping, conspiracy, and extortion charges.

Hewitt found the Reso case to be both an epiphany as well as a frustrating experience. He realized the importance of interagency teamwork and the importance of respecting the boundaries of law enforcement agencies. Hewitt had assumed the Reso case would be the biggest of his career. He was wrong. A brief summer romance in the Poconos at nearby Lake Ariel brought him to Honesdale. He found the lake community refreshing and fell in love with both the area and the girl. But only one lasted. Eventually, he applied to the local Honesdale police department, used some of his FBI connections and was hired some 15 years ago.

However, Hewitt found his job to be routine to the point of boredom, as do most police officers. Some officers turn to alcohol or drugs to alleviate the drudgery of the job. Others overindulge in doughnuts. All three, alcohol, drugs, and doughnuts were temptations easily available on the graveyard shift.

Hewitt consumed strong drink and pastry products in moderation. His solution to job boredom was to enroll in as many law enforcement courses as he could manage. He had been to the State Police training center in Elizabethtown, PA, so many times that he was on the Christmas card list with many of the faculty and staff.

Closing in on 44, Hewitt had remained single and in excellent shape. He believed himself to be better off than many of his colleagues who were divorced or unhappily married. Police work, even in small towns, is tough on marriages. Long hours and revolving shifts do some of the damage. Temptations inherent in working the seamy side of life on the graveyard shift also contribute to the high rate of failure in police marriages.

Hewitt knew of good marriages and bad marriages and it was his considered opinion that while nothing may be better than a good marriage, hell itself offers relief to someone in a bad marriage.

As a single man, he knew that loneliness can be oppressive and deadening, but he was sure that having a person you once loved and who once loved you put most of their energy into making you unhappy had to be worse.

Hewitt had had a major disappointment in love. He had foolishly drifted away from the one woman he had considered marrying, Vivian Modell. She was still single, but was now involved in a serious relationship. Hewitt protected himself from further disappointment, and subconsciously kept himself available for his first love, by focusing on the flaws of every woman his friends and relatives insisted on introducing to him.

This irritated, but did not discourage, his busiest matchmaker, his happily married sister, Colleen. As his cooperation decreased, her aggressiveness increased. Hewitt generally enjoyed spending time with his sister and her husband in their nearby Lake Wallenpaupack lake front home. And he enjoyed babysitting for his two nephews. But Colleen's aggressive search for a mate for her brother had become a source of friction between them until the air was cleared last Thanksgiving.

"Dan, the trouble with you...," began Colleen as she worked on making cranberry butter in the kitchen while her husband and children were camped in front of the TV watching the original *Mighty Joe Young* on Channel 22.

"I know, I know," said Hewitt. "The trouble with me is I'm looking for the perfect woman and no one is perfect. I know, Colleen. We've been over this before."

"And we are going over it again. The woman you want does not exist. Most of the single people I know are too damn critical. All of 'em are looking for Mr. or Ms. Right. But no one, not one of them, is working on making themselves into Mr. or Ms. Right. If you singles were that demanding when it came to purchasing cars, you'd drive every model but you'd all wind up walking everywhere. You put the entire responsibility for the relationship on the other person. That is the opposite of what a relationship is."

"Colleen," said Hewitt. "Please. You're killing me. You've got to stop reading those self-help books, or at least confine their advice to improving your life and leave me alone. I know you don't believe me, but I'm OK with the way things are."

"But are you happy?"

"I'm happier than a lot of married couples we both know."

"That's no answer. I just want you to be happy."

"Then don't hound me about marriage. And please, stop fixing me up. I hate blind dates."

"If I find someone I think you'd like, you're getting her name and number. Call her or don't. That's up to you. But you are getting her number."

"OK, fair enough. But please, no more questions, no more nasty little asides about my marital status."

"What nasty? I'm not nasty."

"Nasty or not, well intentioned or not, the comments are unwelcome and, frankly, boorish."

"Hey, hey, hey. Never call a woman boorish," said Colleen, who had been stung by the remark. She paused and sighed heavily before continuing. "Especially if she is being boorish," she said, reaching over and brushing her brother's cheek. "OK, I'll ease up. No comments, no digs, no inquisition. But if someone comes to mind..."

"Just know I'm getting the number."

All in all, Hewitt was content with his life. On a personal level, there were enough women around; just not the one he wanted. Professionally, he enjoyed being a police officer. With his intelligent approach to the job, and the additional training, Hewitt had become one of the most capable, if underutilized, law enforcement officials in the state.

"Good morning, Curt," said Hewitt to the officer working at one of two desks in the Honesdale PD reception area/waiting room. "Looks like it might clear up today."

"TV says up to three inches of snow," said Curt. "They got that Doppler radar. Can tell you what the weather's like in your own neighborhood."

"They may need Doppler radar to know what the weather is in my neighborhood, but I don't. I look out the window, open the door, there it is, the weather, my neighborhood. Your neighborhood any different?"

"OK, smart guy. They say it's going to snow, but you say it's going to clear up. They got Doppler radar, you don't. So, should I make plans on your say-so, or theirs?"

"What plans? You going on a picnic this afternoon? But I'll stack my record against theirs anytime," said Hewitt.

"So you never listen to the weather," said Curt.

"I may hear it, but unless they are talking about weather that's an hour away, I pretty much ignore it. Haven't you ever noticed how many snowstorms that are in the four-day forecast never arrive?"

"I don't know, I think it is better to be prepared," said Jim.

"Prepared for what? Don't tell me you're one of those snow bunnies that run out and gets milk, eggs, and bread at the first sign of a snowflake."

"You don't want to run out of staples," said Curt.

"What staples. Milk, eggs, and bread are perishables. Why stock up on perishables? What is it with you people? Does the threat of snow create a sudden craving for French toast? You want to be prepared for a bad snowstorm, buy a box of powdered milk and stick it in the cupboard with a few cans of soup. When's the last time a winter storm kept you housebound for days?"

"There was that blizzard in '96 that was a bad one. I was stuck in the house for the better part of two days."

"The worst blizzard in a hundred years and you're stuck in the house for a total of 36 hours-- eating French toast, no doubt."

"By the way, the Chief was asking for you," said Curt.

"And why wouldn't you tell me that instead of wasting my time with small talk about the weather?"

"Well, Detective, maybe I just figured you knew the Chief would want to see you because of the Baby Franco case, it being an unsolved crime and you being such an observant detective and all," said Officer Foley.

"Good point. You know, Curt, there is something really odd about this case. And I don't just mean the missing body. There is something going on here that we haven't uncovered yet. I don't think we've got an accurate sense of what we are dealing with yet. Cover the phones for me while I'm with the Chief. Thanks."

Chief of Police Joseph Wallington was a lifelong resident of Honesdale. His parents owned a modest farm on the edge of town. The day after graduating high school, he signed up for the Marines. His parents were proud of their son as he left on that hot July morning in 1972. He waved goodbye and told them he'd return after boot camp. He returned sooner than that to attend their funeral. According to the newspaper account, Joe's parents, on their way home from Lake Wallenpaupack two weeks after their son had entered the Marines, had a blowout while traveling west on Rt. 6. Joe's father fought to get the car under control, and was able to bring the car to a full stop, but the front end was protruding into the eastbound lane. Before he could ease the car onto the shoulder of the road an eastbound tractor trailer slammed into the front wheel on the passenger's side, spinning the car around and throwing the back end of the car under the rear wheels of the truck, immediately killing Joe's parents.

Joe was granted a 30-day hardship leave to attend the funeral and help straighten out the estate with his older brother and sister. The farm had to be sold to settle the estate.

After boot camp he was assigned to the Military Police in Germany. Upon his release in 1987 his application to the Honesdale Police Department was quickly accepted, in part because of his experience as an MP and because he and his family were well liked in the community.

Now, after 30 years on the force, he was looking forward to retirement. He promised Marge, his wife of 28 years, that he'd retire this year and they would move closer to the children and grandchildren in North Carolina. Truthfully, the lure of fishing in North Carolina was almost as powerful an incentive for moving as were increased visits to the three grandchildren, two girls and a boy.

His impending retirement was undermining his enthusiasm for the job. The chief knew it was time to move on. His style of police work was ill equipped to deal with the mischief-makers, drug dealers, criminals, prosecutors, and defense attorneys of today. The chief's approach to police work was simple. Depending on the situation, he could be more compassionate or much rougher than the younger college-trained cops.

When dealing with kids he knew, the chief was far more likely to give them a lecture than a rap sheet. If they got in trouble again, he'd talk to the kids' parents. Today, a nine-year-old would demand a lawyer if the chief even attempted a lecture.

In his day, a teenage vandal might use a BB gun. Last week a sixth grader brought a .22 pistol to school. It was time for the chief to get out, all right. And today's case, a missing infant corpse from a local funeral home, was just one more sign that something had gone terribly wrong. Let the new guys, like Hewitt, Foley, and Brill deal with today's crazies.

The chief liked Hewitt. As he had said to his wife the night before, "The guy isn't a know-it-all smart ass. Yeah, he goes to a lot of training courses, but he listens, too. We talk about residents, town stories, even old cases. I tell you, I like the guy. I don't know, it's like if I can teach him what I know, then it's like part of me stays on the job."

"Like a father, passing on the family business to his son?" guessed Marge.

"Something like that," said the Chief.

"Will you miss it, Joe?" asked Marge. "If you count the military, you've been at it more than half your life."

"One-hundred-and-fifty-three days, Marge. I've got 153 days left. They can't go by fast enough for me."

Hewitt breezed into the room, rousing the chief from his thoughts.

"Hi, Chief, get much sleep last night?"

"About as much as you. Grab some coffee and a doughnut. Nothing like a sugar boost to get you going."

"Yeah, like this is health food, some kind of energy pill," said Hewitt.

"OK, I decided to pamper myself today," he smiled. "It's gonna be a bitch. There's some sugar behind the doughnut box. There, on the left," said Chief Wallington.

"Any ideas, Joe?" said Hewitt, pouring a cup of coffee but ignoring the doughnuts. "I went over the details last night and I'm still not sure what we have here."

"That makes two of us," said the chief. "Damnedest thing, isn't it? What's your take on Grayson? Whatever happened to that body, I say Grayson's in on it."

"I've got the same feeling, but he had to have help," said Hewitt. "We have at least two suspects, Grayson and the person or persons Grayson gave the body to."

"And money had to be the reason for this."

"Why do you say that?"

"Grayson almost lost the business a few years back. Gambling problem. Thought he had quit, but I checked with

111

my local bookmakers last night. What the hell, it's a small town. We all place bets with the same guys. Anyway, they tell me Grayson's back at it and he took some big hits recently, maybe seven or eight grand."

"Does he owe?"

"No, he's paid up," said the chief.

"But he's desperate for money," said Hewitt.

"Desperate is a strong word. Grayson's no different than most people. Everyone wants more money. Let's just say he needed to recoup on some bad investments."

"OK, he was open to making money on the side," said Hewitt.

"Wide open," said the chief. "But tell me, is there any chance someone stole the body from the funeral home without Grayson's knowledge?"

"I'm not buying that," said Hewitt. "Grayson told me he was going to report the missing body to Officers Foley and Brill once he got the father settled down. But Brill tells me Grayson was trying to get rid of them."

"OK," said the chief. "Grayson's in on it and he had help. But who helped and why?"

"My preliminary list is surprisingly long, could be just about anyone. Here, I need to diagram this," said Hewitt, walking to the whiteboard on the wall to the left of the chief's desk.

"You and your diagrams. Can't you just tell me? And make sure you use an erasable marker. You ruined the last board I had," said the chief.

"This is the way I work, Chief. It helps me see the connections between everyone involved. As for your previous whiteboard, I prefer to say my detective work left an indelible mark on this office."

"Ruined the goddamned board is what you did," said the chief.

"And broke the case, chief. That's worth a $120 whiteboard any day, isn't it?"

"Wasteful is wasteful," said Wallington. "Let's see what you got this time."

"OK," said Hewitt. "I was thinking last night; we need to go back to the beginning of this whole thing. First we have the accident, the Franco woman is in a coma." He scribbled the word, "mother" and then placed a cross next to her name. "Not a suspect, but an important part of the case."

"For this you need a diagram?"

"You'll see. Once we get beyond the accident scene the list of persons connected to this case grows exponentially."

"Does what?" asked the chief.

"It gets long quick. Watch. At the accident scene we have Officer--a township police officer--Cirillo." The felt-tipped marker squeaked on the whiteboard as Hewitt wrote "Accident Scene" on the far left of the board and jotted Cirillo's name underneath. "I haven't talked to Cirillo yet," said Hewitt, "but the township faxed a copy of his report to me yesterday afternoon. According to the report, also at the accident scene were three members of the hospital EMT rescue squad. The squad was headed by Luke McGuinness and two others. I'll just add McGuinness to the EMT squad." Those names were added to the list and Hewitt drew a short stubby arrow directly to the right of the words "Accident Scene". The arrow pointed to the right and at the tip of the arrow he wrote "Hospital". He continued, "Now, at the hospital we've got emergency room personnel. Dr. Smalley, Dr. Johnson, who was just coming on duty, and there had to be nurses on duty, too. I plan to talk to the doctors today. We can get their names then. For now let's list Nurses 1, 2, and 3." Hewitt stepped back to look at the whiteboard, and then moved forward again.

"OK, Chief, then after the emergency room we had three surgical teams that treated the mother. The head injuries led by Dr. Tully, Chief of Neurology; a surgical team that worked on the mother's leg. Dr. Styger led that group. And the OBGYN team headed by Dr. Evans, Chief of Obstetrics. Each of these teams had at least one other physician, an anesthesiologist, and three nurses assigned to it."

"Now what," said the chief?

"Next we have the victim, the baby. She's not really the victim, is she, more like the subject. You know who the victim is?"

"The sleazeball father is the victim," said Hewitt.

"So we make another arrow from the OBGYN team to... 'Baby'. Below the baby we write in the name of the proud papa, and from him we draw an arrow going back to the mother. Now, below the father we include the brains of the outfit, 'Sidney Armstadt, Esquire'. And from him we should have an arrow going to a pot of gold at the end of the rainbow, but we don't have room. There."

"Quite a list," said the chief.

"But wait, there's more," said Hewitt in his best infomercial voice, "We draw an arrow from the baby to...Dr. Nichols, her pediatrician, and from him we have another arrow to...our own, our very own Avery Grayson."

"OK," said the chief, "Let's try this my way for a few minutes. Let's figure out what we know for certain. We know the baby was born, we've got hospital records, and we've got, what, 20 or 30 people at the hospital that can confirm the baby was born."

"OK, incontrovertible fact ne, the baby was born," said Hewitt, writing the word "FACT" as a heading and writing "1. Baby born" under that heading.

"Do we know for a fact the baby was terminally ill? I say yes," said the chief. "I saw that press conference where the doctors, even the hospital administration and hospital lawyer, said the baby was dying. We've got confirmation from too many unimpeachable sources..."

"OK," said Hewitt, writing "2. Baby sick" under the FACT heading.

114

"Now the baby died. We know this is a fact," said the chief, "because we've got the death certificate signed by Dr. Nichols."

Hewitt scribbled "'3. Baby died.'"

"What happened next," asked the chief.

"According to Grayson," said Hewitt, "Dr. Nichols handed over the body to Grayson."

"Anyone else involved in the transfer? Someone from the funeral home, or at the hospital?" asked the chief.

"Not that I know of," said Hewitt. "Grayson didn't mention anyone else."

"So, as far as we know, just Dr. Nichols and Grayson were there for the hand-off, right?"

"Right, Chief."

"Let's concentrate on those two for now," said the chief. "Silva is going to Judge Collins this morning, but he spoke with him last night. Collins is sympathetic. The Wayne County prosecutor's office will be hitting Avery Grayson with a search warrant. Let's see," said the chief, looking at his watch. "Yeah, they should be knocking on Mr. Grayson's door right about now."

"Yeah, Silva called me last night to let me know," said Hewitt. "I was planning to help out at the funeral home..."

"But rather than have you go over there," said the chief, "why not visit Dr. Nichols. Just look how your diagram works out," said the chief, getting out from behind his desk to poke his finger at the whiteboard diagram. "Over on this side, you got scads of people at the accident scene and hospital. Over here, when the kid dies, this is where the rubber hits the road, we got two people, Nichols and Grayson. We agree that Grayson isn't telling us all he knows and we also agree that he had to have help."

"Dr. Nichols might be that help," said Hewitt.

"He might, or who knows," said the Chief, "Grayson might be Dr. Nichols's help. Maybe the body never got to the

115

funeral home. Maybe Dr. Nichols had some other use for it..."

"Medical experiments..."

"Who knows, who cares? We need to have a friendly talk with the good doctor. Then later today we can have a heart to heart with Grayson. He'll be nervous and upset, probably hasn't slept much, and we'll have guys walking out with stacks of boxes. Good time to put a little pressure on him. We might have enough to hold him as a material witness. I don't think he'd hold out long to protect someone else."

"But what's the motive, Chief?"

"Dan, in police work sometimes the motive reveals the crime, and sometimes the crime exposes the motive. My gut tells me we'll be a lot closer to knowing why this happened once we figure out what the hell did happen. Pass me a doughnut."

CHAPTER 9

Joan Evans was sitting up in bed talking with her husband and catching up on the latest news. She was dumbfounded to learn of the strange events surrounding the disappearance of baby Franco. "A cult, some kind of cult," she emphatically stated. As an afterthought she added, "What about the mother?"

Alan smiled. "Believe it or not, there are distinct signs of life. Arm and hand and leg movement. Facial twitching. I was just talking with your friend, Dr. Nichols and he confided in me his astonishment about her recovery. In fact he seemed almost, ah, alarmed and, well, I mean, he wasn't the usual happy, cheerful, positive self he usually is. In fact, I'd say he was downright disappointed and concerned that she might be coming around."

"Disappointed? That's strange, isn't it? Maybe he was just preoccupied about...

"Yeah, preoccupied that she was going to live!"

"But enough about current hospital events, Joan. You look so great, so healthy; you'd never know you had a heart attack. You have color in your cheeks, and...

"And now I need some color in my hair. I must look dreadful to anyone but you, sweetheart," she said.

"But seriously, how do you feel?"

"Fine, energetic..."

"Restful?" he said wondering if she was going to bring up the topic.

"No, Alan. I had that dream again last night. I saw her. She was right before me, right at my bed, like you are right now. She smiled and looked at me." Tears came to Joan's eyes and ran down her cheek. Her lips started to part and her arms shivered. "She said it was OK!"

"OK? What does that mean?"

"I don't know but I can't live with myself knowing, knowing…what I did."

"It was our decision, Joan. We thought it was best. We had so much ahead of us. The decision was ours. We were young, we made a difficult choice. Maybe we didn't know how we'd feel later. We thought we were doing the best thing for us and the baby, ah, the fetus," he pleaded.

"I need to see a priest," Joan finally added. She looked at Alan. "We both need to see a priest." She paused. "Then I want to see Janice Franco."

****

It took the better part of a week for Detective Hewitt to mine the mountain of files removed from the funeral home for the records he wanted--funeral arrangements, paid for by Dr. Frederick Nichols, for three infants who died at Lake Veterans Memorial Hospital while under his care.

All along, Hewitt had been convinced that something other than your typical act of charity was behind these apparent acts of compassionate generosity by Dr.Nichols. Yes, Nichols seemed to be a pious man with deeply held religious beliefs. But Hewitt had known enough religious people to understand that they were just as susceptible to bad judgment and temptations as anyone else.

But Nichols, in Hewitt's mind, didn't seem to be a phony religious zealot who would be found with a floozy in some hotel one day, or who would embezzle hospital funds and run off to Tahiti. He could see the strong-willed, confident Nichols fighting for his perceived moral high ground against all of society. He was the brand of man who would unhesitatingly defy manmade laws whenever they conflicted with his understanding of God's Law.

But is that what had happened in this case? How were Nichols's religious convictions related to the disappearance of an infant's corpse? Were they even related?

118

That was the brain-eater keeping Hewitt awake at night. Bodies, even small bodies, don't just disappear. They are disposed of; in one way or another, for one purpose or another, they are disposed of. If Dr. Nichols was, as Hewitt believed, a man of religious conviction, how could he be involved in trading infant organs or tissue on the black market? And Hewitt was certain Dr. Nichols was not a Jeffrey Dahmer monster putting Swift's modest proposal into action. But to what purpose, consistent with genuine religious conviction, could the body of a dead infant be used?

That was the crux of the problem for Hewitt. Without a use for the body of a dead infant that would be consistent with Dr. Nichols's religious beliefs, Hewitt was either wrong about Dr. Nichols's piety or...

Or what? Hewitt didn't have an "or-what". He was stumped.

He kept going over details of the case. Something about Grayson that told Hewitt the funeral director was a follower, not a leader. Hewitt was certain that it was Dr. Nichols, not Grayson, who was the prime mover in this scheme, whatever it was. Nichols initiated the process. He was the one who brought Grayson in; he was the one who had arranged for infant funerals with Grayson in the past. Maybe Grayson didn't know the whole story, but Nichols did. It was clear to Hewitt by Nichols's entire demeanor. Nichols seemed undisturbed by the fact that the funeral he had paid for had gone terribly wrong. He was comfortable with the fact. He never criticized Grayson, never asked any questions about what Grayson had done with the body. He didn't seem to care. He wasn't curious or concerned, thought Hewitt, because he knew exactly where the body was and why it was there.

Hewitt was examining the funeral home files, certain that they would provide some revealing connection between Baby Franco and the three other infants whose funeral expenses Dr. Nichols had paid. Find that connection, thought Hewitt, and I'll know what the good doctor was up to.

They indicated Nichols had paid all funeral expenses for an infant boy, aged three weeks, in 2004; a six-week-old girl in 2006; and an eight-month-old infant boy in 2010. Hewitt felt he was close to the solution, but he needed more information. He needed the hospital records on those cases. He brought his request to the chief.

"You've hit a dead end, Dan," said Wallington. "But some neighborhoods have dead ends and I think you're in the right neighborhood. But damned if I can figure out what you're on to here."

"I'm not sure either," said Hewitt. "But we've got three other infant deaths--all paid for by Nichols--all handled by Grayson. I don't know what the link may be in this case..."

"So you want to subpoena hospital records on the three infant deaths," said the chief.

"I say all four," said Hewitt. "I want to see those records. There has to be some connection."

"Actually," said the chief, "there doesn't have to be a link. Don't let the answer you want shape the question you ask. It's OK to push an inquiry in one direction or another, but don't force it or you'll only see what you expect to see."

"Aren't you the guy who says that 99 times out of a hundred what's obvious is what's true?"

"Nice to know you listen once in a while. I'm truly flattered. Now tell me, what in this case has been obvious?"

"Damn little."

"Damn right. Nothing has been obvious. So there's a real danger of filling in some of these gaps with a whole lotta 'mighta beens and coulda happeneds'. Now, that's good enough police work for those 99 cases out of a hundred. Most criminals are incredibly unimaginative. But that 100th case, that 1% that represents the really challenging cases, that case will always be beyond you unless you leave the door open for the unexpected. This case here is a genuine bona fide one percenter."

"OK," said Hewitt. "What's next?"

"We call Henry Silva, tell him we want to subpoena the hospital records," said the chief, dialing Silva's direct line. "I'll put him on the speaker phone."

"Silva here," said the voice on the phone.

"Henry, its Joe. Got you on the speakerphone. Detective Sergeant Hewitt is with me."

"Good afternoon, Chief, Detective Hewitt," said Silva cheerfully.

"Afternoon," said Hewitt.

"Henry," said the chief, "here's why we called. It's the Baby Franco case."

"So I assumed," said Silva.

"Right," said the chief. "Dan here has learned, from Dr. Nichols at Lake Memorial that the good doctor arranged to pay all funeral expenses for Baby Franco."

"Unusual, but not criminal," said Silva.

"Well," continued the chief, "Dan has confirmed, through Grayson's records, that Nichols has done this three other times in the past 10 years or so. He's paid the funeral expenses for three infants."

"A generous and compassionate man," said Silva.

"That's a possibility," replied the chief, "but we'd like to have a look at those hospital records to see if there is more to it than that."

"And what are we looking for?" asked Silva.

"Other connections, similarities, links..."

"In other words, Chief, you don't know exactly what you are looking for."

"Tell you as soon as we find it," said the chief.

"Well, at least this time we have a specific and limited request," said Silva.

"So, you won't have to bother Judge Collins..."

"No, chief, I'm sticking with Collins. I need to

121

demonstrate to him that the wiggle room he has given us on the Grayson search has given us some leads, soft as they are. Besides, why give a defense attorney the possibility of asking us why we went to Judge 'A' for some search warrants and Judge 'B' for others? Dan, bring the Grayson files to my office. I'll call Judge Collins now. We should be able to serve the paperwork on the hospital this afternoon."

Silva was as good as his word, but before serving the search warrant on the hospital administrator, Hewitt contacted Vivian Modell. He told himself that this small courtesy was motivated by his desire to remain on good terms with the hospital administration. But seeing Vivian again had revived his old feelings for her. He realized too late that he should have proposed when he had the chance. He thought their age difference would have made a difference, that his "will you marry me" would turn out to be "You're the best guy for me but I want a younger you, and besides I need to spend all my energies finishing law school," but he'll never know because he got her imagined answer stuck in his head and his proposal got lost in his fear. Now she was with Fedderson. His heart still held a beat for Vivian but, well, a lot of buts have washed over the dam. All that aside, Hewitt understood that Fedderson and Vivian could be helpful allies in making a case against Dr. Nichols, if it came to that.

"Dan, I can't tell you how much I appreciate this call," said Vivian. "What time were you planning on serving the search warrant?"

"I've got the papers in hand. I was planning on leaving for the hospital after this call."

"Yes, of course. Do you think you could give me ten or twenty minutes to prepare Doug, I mean Mr. Fedderson? You do whatever you have to do, of course. I'll understand. But if I speak with Mr. Fedderson first, it might facilitate things. Get you in and out quickly and quietly. This would benefit the hospital and your investigation."

"I'll take the scenic route," said Hewitt. "I'll be there in 45 minutes."

"Thank you, Dan. Just go directly to the administrator's office. We'll be waiting."

****

"Vivian," said Fedderson, "This is a surprise," he said as his mind raced to the fact that the break-up was probably one of the best things that could happen. He wondered if he will be again leaving the comfort of his home as Nichols was most assuredly going to have to do. "I wasn't expecting you this afternoon."

"Strictly business, Doug. Your favorite detective is on his way over with a search warrant..."

"Hewitt? Damn. What are our options? What should we do?"

"Here's our options: obey the law and hand over the requested records; challenge the search warrant in court; or you can hide or alter the stuff, which of course is obstruction of justice, very illegal, and not sound legal advice," said Vivian.

"What about the court challenge?"

"On what grounds?"

"Privacy of medical records."

"Don't waste my time, Doug; you've been in hospital administration for years. You must know that the courts have consistently upheld the state's investigative powers in cases like this. We'd delay the process for the length of time it would take to get a hearing. The hearing itself wouldn't last more than 15 minutes. It would be thrown out and I'd probably have to sit through a lecture about bringing frivolous motions before the court. We've got no shot. They've already convinced one judge they have just cause to review the records. It's a small town. Judges don't undermine or embarrass each other. Unless the warrant is seriously

123

flawed, we let it go."

"So what do we do?"

"We don't get a lot of choices here. He hands over the warrant, I check to see that it is in order, we give him what he wants."

"What does he want? Are we going to have cops and prosecutors all over the place? I heard what they did to Grayson's place. Practically put a Mayflower truck in front of the place and filled it up. This will look bad in the papers. God forbid TV crews show up. I won't have some local civil servant damage the reputation of this hospital."

"They aren't going to cause a scene. They are requesting records on three deceased infant patients, from '04, '06, and '10. That's it. Hewitt's the only one coming over. We'll have a clerk pull the files; bring them to your secretary. You go out to her desk, she hands you the files, you come back to your office and hand them to Detective Hewitt, and we're done. No muss, no fuss, no TV, no reporters."

"Why does he want these cases? What have they got to do with the Franco baby?"

"That's the other thing," said Vivian.

"What?"

"Dan says..."

"Dan?"

"Don't be jealous, dear, and strictly professional. He called me as a courtesy. Obviously he wants our cooperation."

"I can see he wants your cooperation."

"This is such an unpleasant side of you, Doug. Unpleasant and, I must say, quite tedious. The fact is he did call and he says Dr. Nichols was the pediatrician on each of these cases..."

"So?" His anxiety level increased.

"...and he paid for Grayson to handle each of the funerals."

"Big deal," he said trying to deflect any legal charges against Nichols. "Dr. Nichols is one of the leading pediatricians in the county and Grayson's Funeral Home handles as many funerals as anyone in this area. So what if Nichols prefers to make arrangements with one home? Besides, we've both known Nichols has done that before. It even came up when Hewitt questioned Nichols here. Nichols told Hewitt about paying for funerals at Grayson's. Hewitt said something about Nichols putting his money where his mouth is."

"I remember," said Vivian. "You thought Hewitt was being complimentary. But I told you he was up to something."

"So why would he want those records? He already knows Nichols was involved."

"You're looking at this like a hospital administrator," said Vivian.

"Well, duh..."

"Douglas, this is not a wholesale fishing expedition. They are looking for the medical records of three deceased patients."

"So..."

"Well," said Vivian, "it is clear to me that the investigation is centered on Grayson and Nichols."

"Maybe it's clear to you because it's clear to Hewitt."

"Doug, somehow even though that doesn't make any sense, it is nonetheless, quite insulting."

"But Vivian," argued Fedderson, "you know what kind of man Dr. Nichols is."

"Do I?"

"Oh, come on, Vivian. Can you see him involved in some body snatching conspiracy? You may find him a little hard to take sometimes when it comes to religion, but, really, you can't believe he'd be involved in something like this. I don't care if your old flame does think Dr. Nichols is a Dr. Mengele. I don't think you should be favoring the police over the hospital's interests in this matter."

"OK, that's it. My past relationship with Detective Hewitt has nothing to do with the advice I have been attempting to offer here. You don't seem to be able to get over it. I suppose this was bound to happen sooner or later."

"What?"

"We both knew it was a bad idea to get involved while we also have this professional relationship," said Vivian. "We've had a moratorium on seeing each other socially since that damn Franco woman drove her car off of Route 6. But it hasn't helped."

"I can see where this is going," said Fedderson.

"Well good for you. It's the first damn thing you've been able see clearly since you met Hewitt."

"So, we're done then. That's it. Or just until all this blows over," said Fedderson.

"No, Doug, we need a clean and complete break here," said Vivian. "It is too much of a distraction for both of us. Once we're done with this Dr. Nichols investigation I'll turn over the hospital files to a partner in the firm."

"If that's the way you want it..."

She paused. "Doug, there were so many good, no great times. You're a great guy, you made me feel important, but, honestly, there was… Well, to answer your question, I think it is best," said Vivian.

He nodded. "So now what?"

"Well," said Vivian, "I think we can agree that Nichols is high on Hewitt's list for now and we need to keep that in mind. We should just hand over the records. There is no reason to tell Detective Hewitt what a good and decent man Dr. Nichols is."

"What's the point of that? I mean, Dr. Nichols is a good and decent man," said Fedderson.

"First of all, it won't change a thing. Hewitt is still going to look through the files and make up his own mind about Nichols. Second, you don't want to create the impression that you have an undue interest in this case. Interests that would, say, cause you to be less than cooperative. If Hewitt suspects we are siding with Dr. Nichols, he may not be as helpful as he has been. Remember he did tip us off about the search warrant. He could have just popped in here, served the papers regardless of who else was around and then gone on his merry way."

"I'm ever so grateful to Detective Hewitt."

"He's got his job to do, we've got ours," said Vivian.

"Well, do we tell Dr. Nichols?"

"Have you been listening to me at all? These are hospital records. We are under no obligation to advise Dr. Nichols of the search warrant. Besides, officially, we don't know that Nichols is the subject of the investigation," said Vivian.

"Not much advantage in having this inside information if you can't use it," said Fedderson. "They're serving us with the warrant, we can tell anyone we want about it. I say, since these were his patients, he should be told."

"They served us because they don't want him to know what they are looking into. Look, nothing good can happen by tipping off Dr. Nichols. Say he's done something illegal, you warn him and he might be tempted to cover his tracks, destroy records. That could expose us to obstruction of justice charges. How does that help the hospital? If he's done nothing wrong, these records can't hurt him. But the greater threat to us is pissing off the investigators and the prosecutor's office. They have been very solicitous of us so far. Why risk losing that cooperation?"

"So we hang one of our doctors out to dry just so we don't upset Hew..," Fedderson paused in mid-sentence and continued along a safer path. "Just to please the prosecutor's office? I don't like it, Vivian."

"Let's keep this on a strictly professional level," said Vivian slowly. "As the attorney representing this hospital it is my professional opinion that the hospital would be best served by responding to the search warrant and not involving ourselves in the matter any further."

"No call to Dr. Nichols."

"That is my professional advice to you," said Vivian curtly.

The phone rang. Fedderson picked it up. "Yes, we've been expecting him. Send Detective Hewitt in," said a weary Doug Fedderson.

After the files had been given to Hewitt and Vivian had returned to her office, Fedderson called Dr. Nichols and told him exactly which files had been taken. He then phoned Philip Duran.

****

Hewitt placed the files on his desk. He poured himself a cup of coffee before he started reading. The infants whose brief and painful lives were documented in the medical files that Hewitt had been studying for three hours had several things in common. All were under the care of Dr. Nichols. Grayson's Funeral Home handled the arrangements, and Dr. Nichols paid for the funerals.

Nothing new there.

Two more facts struck Hewitt. All three were born with severe complicated infant illnesses, and in each case the parents had authorized the modification of medical treatment, no heroic measures to save the child. In fact, no measures at all. The parents of all three infants had chosen to let the children die rather than suffer for weeks, months, or years only to succumb to a relentless terminal illness.

Hewitt slowly walked around his desk, meandering among the obstacle course of sloppily stacked files to the left, right, and rear of his chair. The desktop was cluttered with open manila folders. Several folders bore rings of coffee stains, the hallmark of late night work in a cluttered office. The office was dark, except for Hewitt's desk lamp.

He removed the contents of his in-box absentmindedly, looked at the label of each item, tossed a few into the wastepaper basket, and stopped to open the letter from Alan Evans, husband Dr. Joan Evans.

"Son of a bitch," he said to himself as the contents of the letter soaked in. "Now it makes sense. It's crazy, but it makes sense. It's consistent at least. Damn."

The detective circled his desk nervously three times before dialing Vivian Modell's home phone number.

"Hello."

"Yes--Vivian," said Hewitt. "It's Dan."

"Dan, my goodness. It's been some time since you've called me at all, and today I get two calls from you."

"This is business, Vivian..."

"Ah, well, I would be shocked were it anything but. How can I help?"

"Can you tell me if Steve Williams, you know--the father--or his attorney ever agreed to withdraw medical treatment for Baby Franco? There have been some rumors..."

"Is this on the record or off?"

"Just between us tonight. Tomorrow I'll attempt to confirm the information elsewhere without involving you. What I can't prove I can't use. I just need a little direction here."

"Armstadt, the alleged lawyer, had made some noise about authorizing modification of treatment. Doug was going to bring it to the board and then the child, mercifully, and luckily, died."

"Why mercifully?"

"The poor child's suffering aside, this was a messy issue for Doug and the board. I'm sure it's no surprise to you that there was a suggested *quid pro quo*, something that can be done in a small town, provincial setting, you understand."

"Armstadt wanted what?" asked Hewitt.

"We're still off the record?"

129

"Same deal as before," said Hewitt.

"It was never stated in so many words, but the basic deal was clear. The father authorizes cessation of treatment, the baby dies, and the hospital saves thousands of dollars..."

"Armstadt wanted a cut of the resulting savings?"

"And the money left in the charity fund," said Vivian.

"Anything in writing?" asked Hewitt.

"We've got a letter of agreement stating that the hospital would not hold Williams liable for payment of hospital bills for Baby Franco or her mother, unless his net worth exceeds $400,000 in the next three years."

"Protecting the windfall."

"That was my take on it," said Vivian.

"Anything in writing on withdrawal of treatment..."

"No. Armstadt was smart enough not to make a direct verbal request either. It was all hints and suggestions. He would occasionally ruminate aloud that the hospital would save a lot of money if the poor child were no longer suffering, i.e., if she died. Believe me, it was all very clear, yet there's no way to prove he ever made a direct offer."

"Was the board going to go for it?"

"It's in no one's interest for me to speculate on that," said Vivian. "The whole question became moot once the baby died."

"Did, ah, did Dr. Nichols know?"

"Doug Fedderson told him. He has a surprisingly high regard for Dr. Nichols. And as you know Nichols is a strident pro-life advocate. He strongly disagreed with withdrawing routine treatment. But Mr. Fedderson felt Dr. Nichols should know about it before the board made a decision. To prepare him, I guess."

"What's this Mr. Fedderson stuff," said Hewitt, "I thought you two were..."

"Look, I don't need a detective nosing around in my private life."

"OK, OK. Didn't mean to pry," said Hewitt. "I do

appreciate the information."

"Forget it," said Vivian, "it's been a tough couple of days. How about helping out an old pal? How much trouble is Nichols in?"

"Off the record?"

"Completely."

"If my hunch is right, he's got problems. Possible Federal charges," said Hewitt.

"Federal?"

"Kidnapping."

CHAPTER 10

Father Charles sat at the bedside of Joan Evans. The 81-year old Jesuit was substituting for the regular hospital chaplain that month. He looked forward to spending part of his summer vacation at the hospital. He enjoyed the lakeland atmosphere and relaxing summer attitude of the vacationers. Although he missed the "rough and tumble" penitent from his weekend assignment parish in Newark, NJ, he appreciated being God's servant in the vacationing region where the confessions usually were not soul searching enough or sufficiently dire to ask the penitent for more than three "Hail Marys'" or maybe, an "Our Father and a Glory Be..." And typically even in the case of an end of life soul searching confession the guilt was more of a re-hash of sorrows and previous forgiven sins.

Oftentimes, Father Charles saw his clerical role as more of a counselor than priest and his task was more to reassure the individual that past sins were already forgiven and that his grace infused life really meant more to others than he believed. "Enough of this George Bailey 'my life is a waste' mentality," he'd think to himself. "I'm a priest," he'd tell his parishioners and associates, "and the seven sacraments are my truest of friends, my own personal encounter with the Almighty and all of them are capable of taking me to the most adventurous of places, especially the inner workings of a man's soul, especially my own." He treasured any moment he was able to mingle and rejoice among God's people sacramentally.

Alan was also in the room. Fr. Charles felt ill at ease at first. He sensed something more monumental than initially appeared was going to take place, more than the usual penance was about to unfold. He smiled as he placed his well-worn and tattered penitential stole over his shoulders. He was concerned because both husband and wife wanted him to hear their joint confession. "I haven't experienced a couple's confession for a long time," he said with a smile and nervous laugh. "One's sins are a private matter between you and God. Are you certain you want each other to experience the promptings of the spirit in the souls of each other?"

Joan and Alan smiled and nodded," Yes."

Fr. Charles continued, "The sacrament is restorative and often more revealing about one's psyche than a person wants to accept or even reveal to another, especially to a spouse. Some marriages can't cope with that much openness. Truth is beauty and sometimes very stressful on a relationship. But always its God's blessing of the moment." They smiled at each other.

"Courage," Charles thought to himself. He looked at them. He asked, "Is this some kind of marriage encounter practice?"

"Marriage encounter, Father?" she asked. "I don't understand."

"35 to 40 years ago…Oh never mind, I'm much older than you. I mean hearing two confessions at the same time…but that was then and this is now!"

Nervously, Joan began. "I don't know to categorize it as a sin, if it is a sin, or, or, or something else. It was years ago, I was in school before I met Alan…" She paused, reflected, and started crying. The tears freely ran down her cheeks. Alan held her hand as he reached for a handkerchief. Handing it to her she blurted, "I had an abortion. I thought I was doing the right thing. I thought my conscience was right, the decision seemed so right, so legal. Yes, it was legal; the Supreme Court said it was OK. But even then, it didn't seem right, moral," She paused touching the stitches in her chest. She smiled as she thought about the baby, Eve. "I didn't commit a crime. I didn't want to have a child at that time." She paused and took a reflective breath. "Sometime in the future, at a later time, but not then," she said wanting to justify her youthful decision to

133

her older, more understanding self. She paused. "I'm not trying to look good or sugar coat my actions, Father Charles, but I want you to know my state of mind at the time. Is that OK with you? I don't want to justify the action, but I think I am. Am I rambling, Father? I don't mean to. I just want to say it all, completely."

"Don't concern yourself with getting all the facts correct, my child, just tell me what's on your mind and we'll trust the Lord to sort it all out. He's the master at doing such things…I'm a mere sounding board," he smiled. The elderly priest smiled and nodding his head reassured her that sometimes it was best to ramble. He again reminded her that in a heartfelt ramble sometimes the truth squeezes through the soul and eventually takes a shape of its own and comes out in staccato-like words and phrases. He patted her hand and smiled at Alan.

"I could barely afford school costs and didn't have any extra money to raise a child. I wanted more out of life."

Alan reached for the open soda can on the bedside table and poured her a glass of ginger ale. She sipped and continued. "I wanted to have a child at the right time…when I could afford the baby emotionally and financially. Maybe even have a house before having a family. Marry the right man," she heartfelt admitted as she looked at her tearful understanding husband.

Joan regained her composure. "After all, the nurses at the clinic and the doctor said it would be 'OK'". And it was at first. I mean, I felt, well, good about the whole thing, relieved in a way, as though I joined some kind of 'You go, girl!' club," as she pumped her fist in the air.

"I never saw the baby. I was only pregnant a few months. They said it was deformed, a Trisomy-21 baby and that it was best for me and everyone I love that I didn't give birth. I'm a physician now and know better…that even if my child was a Trisomy-21, that's Down Syndrome, Father, that her life would have been fantastically full. The clinic staff was positive that it would die in a few months, that there was no way to keep the baby alive. They told me that my baby would suffer. Then they congratulated me in a wise decision. But, Father, my decision was made out of fear. I mean I didn't know absolutely if my baby was deformed or would be sick, or would die, or would life a full life. I wanted to justify the whole thing by believing them. I didn't care. I just didn't want the baby. I didn't want the bother. What would my parents say? I was ashamed and burdened. And the problem now is that it felt right then and there to abort the baby. But it doesn't feel right now. In fact I see the baby in my dreams…and the baby waves and smiles at me. My God..," she screamed. "Then I wake up and look around and sometimes cry. I want that child. I'm so sorry for what I've done. Can God ever forgive me? But why should he? I can't forgive me," she screamed aloud crying.

Minutes later Alan added, "I met Joan several years later, Father. But in a way, crazy as it seems I know…it seems like I'm part of her abortion. In a heavenly or cosmic way, since all things are present to the Almighty, it seems that my meeting Joan and her abortion are spiritually linked somehow. A sin of bad timing in not meeting her before she got pregnant, some kind of a sin of omission… After all I am my brother's keeper and do I share in his sin?"

The priest walked to the open hospital room door and softly closed it. He returned to his chair and reflected. "The mercy of God is unfathomable. The sacrifice of Jesus atoned for every sin no matter when, how connected to another, how deep, how vile, how repulsive, or how often. For God not to understand the circumstance, the connectivity, the relevance of heavenly forever with the ticking of time…for God not to forgive is to lessen the sacrifice of his son. How could a father deny the love of his son and how could a son reject the love of a father? To think differently is wrong, is heresy."

Joan nodded to Alan and continued talking…

135

****

The next day Prosecutor Henry Silva was in his office at 6:30 a.m. making coffee in preparation for his meeting with Hewitt and Chief Wallington. Hewitt had called the Wayne County prosecutor and the police chief the night before requesting the early morning meeting. He outlined his theory to each, and all agreed to consider the next step at this early morning meeting.

Mr. Coffee had just begun to sputter when Hewitt and the chief arrived.

"Mr. Prosecutor, where the hell are you," shouted Chief Wallington in a voice exuding false irritation.

"Back here, in the kitchen, you old goat. You know the way back here better than you do to any room in the courthouse, except maybe the men's room, or the concession stand that's always filled with doughnuts," answered Silva.

"Not only a great legal mind, but the man makes coffee too," said Wallington. "How's it going, Henry?"

"Fine, just fine, coffee will be ready in a minute, boys. How you doing, Hewitt? Think you've got a tiger by the tail on this one, do you?"

"Not sure what I've got, but it sure isn't your typical case."

"That it is not," said Silva. "All right then, what say we get started? Detective..."

"Yes, sir. Well, I want to outline a suspicious pattern that involves three previous incidents with a number of disturbing similarities with the Baby Franco case. OK. Nichols had offered to pay for the funeral costs of the Franco funeral at Grayson's. He also paid for the Grayson Funeral Home to handle the funerals of three other infants who died while in his care."

"Right," said the Chief. "Nichols has said as much himself. It's a matter of the hospital public record."

"Yes, he has," said Hewitt. "He also says he's done this

136

all through his career. But for now, I want to focus on the four local incidents."

"Go on," said Silva.

"Another similarity is in each case is the patient's family had decided to modify or discontinue treatment. Essentially, they had decided it would be better for the infant to die quietly and with dignity than to continue suffering," said Hewitt. "As far as we know, that is the only time Dr. Nichols has paid for funeral arrangements in Honesdale. He certified that he was present when each child died. In each case he was the person, the "who" who contacted the medical examiner to sign off on the death certificate."

"As you would expect the attending physician to do…," said Silva. "Routine, state mandated and state regulations," he added.

"Yes, but every one of these deaths occurred between the hours of one and 3 a.m." said Hewitt. "And each time the body was literally handed to Grayson by Dr. Nichols less than an hour after the reported death. None of these bodies spent any time in the hospital or county morgue."

"And you're saying there were no other witnesses, no one else involved when the body was transferred?" asked Silva.

"No one, no nurse, another doctor or ambulance driver, an orderly, night cleaning crew? You're sure?" asked Wallington.

"Nope. It was an early morning transfer every time, directly from Dr. Nichols to Grayson, no others were involved."

"I can see where that might sound suspicious," said Silva, "but really, what would you expect? Graveyard shift, skeleton crew, makes sense no one else was there."

"Yes but for all four deaths to occur just when there would be so few witnesses…"

"Like he could control the time of death…." said Silva, "or are you saying he killed these infants. Why would he?

137

From what I understand they were dying already. Just a matter of time."

"No I don't think he killed them, but I am sure he didn't want any witnesses around either. He was very careful to make sure there were none," said Hewitt.

"Why?" asked Wallington.

"Because I don't think the bodies were handed over to Grayson."

"So you said last night," said Silva. "So what's your theory about what he did with these four dead infants?"

"You're getting ahead of me, Mr. Prosecutor. "I'll answer all your questions, but let me lay the groundwork first."

"OK, but so far all I've heard is a string of coincidences that a rookie public defender could win on reasonable doubt."

"I do have this," said Hewitt, handing Silva a letter and medical chart, "Alan Evans, Dr. Evans' husband sent them to me." He paused, "By the way, she's recovering nicely, I understand. Time in the hospital seems to grow on her, we'll get a sworn deposition from her when she's up to it," he smiled as he looked at the others.

"Rather than read these now," said Silva, "give me the short version. What do these prove?"

"The medical chart addendum was signed by Dr. Evans and written the day before Baby Franco supposedly died. According to this chart, the baby's condition had not changed much in weeks."

"And this is significant because…" interjected Silva.

"Because," said Hewitt, "The chart prepared by Nichols hours later indicated the baby was on the brink of death."

"It would seem that Dr. Nichols was right," said Silva.

"Dr. Evans didn't think so; she believed Nichols was deliberately falsifying the infant's medical records."

"Why?" asked Silva.

138

"To make it look like the baby was dying."

"Which it did," said Silva.

"No, it didn't," insisted Hewitt. "That's the whole thing. Baby Franco didn't die that night. She might even still be alive."

"Ridiculous," said Silva.

"Hear the boy out, Henry," interjected the chief. "I think he's on to something here. Just hear him out."

"By all means, Detective, please continue."

"This investigation was going nowhere because we were all stuck on one thing," said Hewitt, "what happened to the body? Who would want it, and why? It just didn't make sense. But if there were no corpse, if the baby did not die, the pieces fit."

"Put them together for me, would you detective," said Silva.

Hewitt scratched his chin and took a deep breath.

"Faking the infant's death would be perfectly consistent with Dr. Nichols's save-a-life, pro-life convictions. The hospital environment was a threat to the child, the father was about to authorize the hospital to discontinue treatment. So he faked her death..."

"And then what?" demanded Wallington.

"After faking the death he handed the baby over to someone else's care."

"But why on earth would he do that, Dan? This is starting to sound preposterous. What's his motivation?" asked Wallington.

"He's a fanatic," said Hewitt, "in Nichols mind, discontinuing treatment is the same as murder."

"So he just ignores the wishes of everyone else involved with the case..." said Silva.

"He'd have no problem with that," said Hewitt. "To him, faking the death all the deaths, giving them over to someone else to care for, would be doing God's will. He thinks in those terms"

139

"So the undertaker..." said Wallington.

"Grayson never saw those bodies," said Hewitt. "At the funerals the coffins were empty. When Steve Williams insisted on seeing his daughter, Grayson was forced to stick a doll in the box to try to fool him. I'm telling you, he buried empty coffins. We get an exhumation order for the three other deaths, put three empty coffins in front of Grayson and he'll tell us everything he knows. He'll give us Nichols, guaranteed."

"So you want me to go to Judge Collins..." began Silva.

"I don't care who we go to..." said Hewitt.

"...and get a court order allowing us to dig up the graves of three infants."

"Yes, sir," answered Hewitt. "That's what I think we need to do to wrap up this case."

"And if you are wrong?" asked Silva.

"I don't think I'm wrong," said Hewitt. "It all fits--the withdrawal of treatment; the conflicting medical charts; the lack of witnesses at the early morning transfer of the bodies; avoiding the hospital morgue, which is right down the hall to the right in the hospital, I remind you...again so there would be no witnesses; using Grayson agreeing to pick up the bodies immediately. Dr. Nichols's life convictions. It all fits. We've got motive, we've got opportunity..."

"At best, it's all circumstantial," said Silva.

"Until we bring up the empty coffins," countered Hewitt."

"If they are empty," said Chief Wallington, shifting in his chair. "Dan, sometimes when we think all the pieces fit together it's only because we don't have a complete picture of what we're looking at. Like those blind men feeling an elephant, you know, where one thinks an elephant is round like a tree because he's got a hold of the elephant's leg and the other guy thinks the elephant is skinny like a rope 'cause he's holding onto the tail. It all fits for them, too, but ain't no elephant that looks like a tree or a rope."

"That's why we need this exhumation order. It keeps coming back to that," said Hewitt.

"Dan," said Silva, "exhumation is a serious step. Courts don't do this lightly. And this involves infant deaths, dammit, Dan. What judge is going to want to risk a wrong call on something like this?"

"I'm not taking this lightly," said Hewitt.

"Didn't say you were, Dan," said Silva. "My point is that a judge is going to be very careful before allowing us to exhume infant graves."

"So what do we do now?"

"With that contradictory medical chart, I think we've got a half-decent circumstantial case here. I'll take it to Judge Collins, but I won't push hard. If he won't go for it we'll have to try something else."

"Like what?" asked Hewitt.

"Hell, we put a little more pressure on Grayson," said the Chief. "We haven't really begun to lean on him. We bring him in for questioning, mention these three other cases during the course of our conversation, and see what happens. If he turns on Nichols and says he never got the bodies, well then, it would be a simple matter to get that court order."

"Should we squeeze Grayson first then, and if he turns on Nichols, go to Collins?" asked Hewitt.

"And if he doesn't turn, then what, we've got less to go on," said Silva. "No, you've made a decent case here. I'll go to Collins with it, and see what happens. He may turn us down now, but if Grayson comes around, the judge will come through."

****

"Henry, Henry, you're killing me here," said Judge Collins as he paced from one side of his chambers to the other. The seated prosecutor turned from side to side in his chair to keep the tall thin judge in sight.

"Judge, we've got a strong case here. Those graves are empty," said Silva.

"Fine, you're sure, but it's my name on the court order. Damn. Infants no less. The death of a child, Henry, that's the kind of emotional wound that never heals. I've experienced it in my own family. My daughter lost a six-month-old son. It is hard enough for these families to put their lives back together again. And you want me to bring all those painful memories back to those poor families..."

"I'm sorry, Judge, I didn't know..."

"SIDS, Sudden Infant Death Syndrome. Tore up the entire family. My daughter's troubles all began with her son Eric's death. Her marriage eventually fell apart, each blaming the other, all those "what if's". It's not like my wife and I could help much with them living out west in Denver. There was so much we didn't know at the time. It was their combined sense of guilt as if they had done something wrong and, oddly enough, an overwhelming sense of shame. She started drinking heavily to hide from the embarrassment of her son's death. Her husband would call her on it…then came the accusations, it all fell apart. You know about the accident."

"Yes, I remember Judge. A shame. Just a terrible shame, but I didn't know the circumstances surrounding it."

"Yes. A shame. Still, I'm not supposed to let any of that influence me. I'm a judge. Officer of the court. My job is to adjudicate the law, not apply personal standards. Bullshit. I'll apply the law as I understand it, and my understanding is influenced by what life has taught me. And in this case, it taught me about hard personal heartache. Suffice to say, I'm not going to cause pain to those families by disturbing those graves unnecessarily."

"But Judge, we need the exhumation order, "he pleaded. "Yes, the families are important, but what about the greater community? This is a disturbing case. People are upset. There's a lot of fear and mistrust out there. Some blame the hospital; others Grayson, there are even rumors of cult

142

sacrifices, goblins, the devil himself active and living in the deep waters of Lake Wallenpaupack. If we are right, and we exhumed just one of the graves we could break down Nichols and Grayson and get to the bottom of this. And we've got that conflicting medical chart."

"Medical chart, humph," mused Collins. "Henry, how long you been at this game?"

"Long enough to know what you're going to say next."

"That's right, you know as well as I that we could get ten doctors to examine a patient and we could get ten different charts."

"Judge, you can't ignore the case we've built here."

"The hell I can't. I'm a judge; I can ignore any damn thing I want to. I could ignore you too, but I won't. Henry, tell you what I'll do. I'll call the families..."

"Dammit, Judge, why put yourself through that? You don't have to..."

"I know I don't have to. We've been over that. But I'm going to talk to those families, as a courtesy. Even a judge can be courteous. I'm going to ask their permission to do this. If one says OK, I'll sign the order; otherwise, you get that young detective of yours to get me more evidence."

"Judge," said Silva, "that could take days."

"What's the hurry? Where's the harm in waiting? Your supposed evidence will stay put. You afraid someone's going to dig up those graves and stick bodies in them? Give me the names of those families. I'll have my aide start making those calls today. But I'm telling you, Henry, if the family chooses not to cooperate, I'm not going to force them unless you get me some hard cold facts."

"Like Grayson admitting he didn't get the bodies?"

"If he says he didn't receive any of those bodies, you won't have to wait long for my signature on the exhumation order."

****

143

Two days later, Joan Evans was beginning to feel her old self again. She had confided to Alan that since their confession with Fr. Charles, she felt "renewed, like an overdue library book." He laughed at her horrible example of the grace of the sacrament of penance, but understood her feeling. Later that morning, Laura Rankin, the surgeon who successfully completed the by-pass, was sitting on the edge of her bed.

"I've been told that you have been lurking around the nurses' station lately, no doubt reviewing my progress notes on your chart," Laura began. "Do you concur with my notations?" she asked laughing.

"Your handwriting is so legible, Laura. I can see you excelled at the Palmer Method! But yes, I concur. I'm feeling very, ah, healthy, and ready for the next step."

"Which is…?"

"Getting to know Janice Franco as well as possible. I think I want to be more a part of her life. I think there is a connection," she confided to her friend.

"Sounds like she can use a friend."

"And, again as odd as it may seem, I'm curious about the good Dr. Fred Nichols. There might be more to him than I'm giving him credit for. It might be time for me to review all the relationships in my life, the new post penance me, that is."

****

Three days had passed. The judge had spoken with two families. Both strenuously objected to the exhumation. Judge Collins had informed the prosecutor's office of each refusal and Henry Silva decided it was time to step up the pressure on Avery Grayson.

Grayson was asked to come to the county courthouse complex for questioning. "Am I under arrest?" he had asked when Hewitt called.

"No, Avery, technically you are being detained for questioning."

"About?"

"Well, Avery, the Baby Franco case...."

"You've questioned me about that before."

"Well, we've got a few new questions and of course there are these three other related matters," said Hewitt.

"Three other related matters, what related matters?"

"Avery," said Hewitt, "we'll explain all that to you when you get down here. Do you want us to send a patrol car to pick you up?"

"No, no. I'm on my way. Holy hell, please, no patrol cars. Can I have my attorney there? I want my attorney present."

"It's your right..."

"I'm going to call him and then I'll get down there."

"You can call him from here, if you like, Avery," said Hewitt.

"No, that's OK. I'll take care of it."

"OK, Avery, we expect to see you here within the hour. If not, we'll be forced to put out a warrant for your arrest," said Hewitt.

"Warrant, what for?"

"If I'm in a good mood, I could issue a warrant naming you as a material witness to a crime. But I doubt I'd be in a good mood if you were late," said Hewitt.

"So what are you saying?"

"I'm saying it is in your best interests to be here within the hour."

Avery hung up and made his frantic phone call to his attorney, Ralph Fitzmorris. Fifteen minutes later Grayson arrived at Fitzmorris's office.

"Did they give any indication what they wanted to discuss?" asked Fitzmorris.

"The Franco case and three others..."

"Others. What others, Avery?"

"I'm a dead man. I'm totally a dead man. A dead man."

"Avery, for me to do the best possible job as your attorney, I've got to know everything. Everything."

"What can you do for me? I'm a dead man. We've got to be there in 45 minutes or they're going to arrest me."

"Avery, the difference between good legal advice and great legal advice is knowing when to cut the best possible deal. I can't do that unless you tell me exactly what's been going on. Let's use the time we have left to your best advantage."

"Yeah, it's time you heard everything..."

****

As Grayson told his story to Fitzmorris, Grace Bedford reached for the ringing phone in her modest Hawley apartment.

"Mrs. Bedford?"

"Speaking."

"Grace Bedford?"

"Yes."

"Mrs. Bedford, this is Diane Huffman calling from the courthouse, I'm Judge Everett Collins's personal assistant. I'm phoning from his chambers on the second floor. The judge has some questions for you. If you have a moment, would you please take a call from the Judge Collins."

"Sure," was the only response the stunned 29-year-old brunette could muster.

"Mrs. Bedford, this is Judge Everett Collins..."

"I'm sorry, but I don't understand. Judge Collins? What do you want? I'm sorry. That sounded rude. I'm a little flustered, the courthouse? Judges don't usually call here. What can I do for you?"

"Well, Mrs. Bedford, I want to discuss a delicate matter with you, and I want to begin by telling you that you are under no obligation to approve anything. We can meet at the courthouse or your home if you wish. You may even have your attorney present; although I don't think it is necessary. The conversation will be off the record, just between you and me."

"No, now is OK. But, I'm sorry, Judge, I have no idea what this is about."

"I'm calling about your son, Greg..."

"Greg? My son, Greg? He died a long time ago, Judge. June 30 is his anniversary. He was just a baby. Why would you be calling me about him? And, why now? It's been a long time, so much has happened."

"Yes, I'm aware of the date of your son's death. And that's the reason for my talking with you. You might be able to add some sorely needed information to an ongoing criminal investigation. And forgive me; I really can't get more specific than that at this time. The police have advised me that your family could help in the investigation."

"How?"

"The police have asked me for a court order to allow the medical examiner to examine Gregory."

"Oh, my God! But how, he's buried in the cemetery." She stopped and then processed the magnitude of the request. "You want to dig up my baby!"

Without skipping a beat the judge quickly interjected, "Madam, I understand how painful this must be for you. I know what you are going through. My own daughter had a similar tragic loss several years ago. But, in your case the police have presented a credible case of wrongdoing and I am asking for your permission to help us."

"Did somebody kill my baby?"

"No, Mrs. Bedford, nothing like that. There was nothing anyone could do to help your son. I am sorry to have to ask you to help us. But I did not want to authorize any court order to proceed with the exhumation of your loved one without first speaking to you."

There was silence and Collins could hear the heavy breathing and sobbing at the other end of the phone.

Compassionately he added, "I'm sorry to have to ask you this permission, Mrs. Bedford, but there is no other way…"

"Do I have to be there?"

"No, Mrs. Bedford. No."

"What will they do? They won't cut him up."

"No, nothing like that. You have my word. They only want to inspect the casket, only the casket," he emphasized.

"And when they are done?"

"They will return him to his resting place with clergy present and with dignity, I'll see to it personally."

Again, silence.

"You said your daughter lost a child, Judge?"

"Yes, Mrs. Bedford. A boy. Eric. He was four months old. SIDS…Sudden Infant Death Syndrome."

"Yes, I know what SIDS is. Four months old, you say?"

"He was our daughter's only child," he responded not wanting to go deeper into the resulting family tragedy. He realized this call was about Mrs. Bedford's son, not his family tragedy.

"My Gregory was eight months, but we hardly ever had him at home. He was very sick you know, right from the beginning. We tried helping him. They helicoptered him to the Children's Hospital in Philadelphia, they call it CHOP."

"Yes, I'm familiar with it."

"He had the best of care but he was sick, so sick. They tried and the more they tried helping him the more we hoped he would respond. Finally, they said nothing more could be done. The hospital sent him home. He developed a fever and I took him to Lake Memorial, but they couldn't do anything to help him…" she said until her voice dropped to a whisper. "Will doing this help anyone?"

"I believe so, Mrs. Bedford. If you say 'yes', some good can come of this." He felt her anguish. He felt the pain of her memory and her worse pain of all…the pain of unrequited hope. It takes every ounce of strength out of a person to have that much hope in the face of an unforgiving illness of a loved child. He wondered how he would have fared if Eric had some other fatal disease for a long time before his death. Maybe the merciless axe of SIDS was the best Eric could muster to spare the family the pain of unrealistic expectations.

"It's OK, Judge. You tell them it's OK. Just make them be gentle," she said sobbing.

"Yes, Mrs. Bedford, I will. Thank you. Oh, by the way, I'll ask my assistant to stop by your home later today. Will you be available to sign some documents for me? "

"Yes, I'm home, anytime later today is fine. And Judge, if your daughter needs someone to talk to, she can call me. There's this local support group. I still go. Talking hurts, but it helps, too. You know what I mean. I can tell you understand."

"I believe I do, Mrs. Bedford. A very compassionate offer. Thank you."

"You're welcome. God bless. Goodbye."

Judge Collins paused briefly before dialing his secretary's extension. "Diane, I don't want to be disturbed for the next 20 minutes," said the judge, holding back his tears. He removed his glasses and wept.

****

Avery Grayson sat with his attorney, Ralph Fitzmorris, at a long table across from Detective Hewitt. The table was in the center of a 10-foot x 14-foot brown paneled room in the county prosecutor's expanse within the county courthouse complex. Foot traffic had worn thin the off-green industrial carpet that had witnessed the confessions of many individuals who cried and pleaded for mercy within the walls of the "box". A one way glass mirror was in the middle of one of the longer walls. A door was on the adjacent wall. A picture of the American flag was firmly affixed next to a flag of the Commonwealth of Pennsylvania near the door. At one end of the table a court stenographer sat silently and typed every word spoken in the room. A video recorder was focused on Grayson. Hewitt walked to the unit and peered into the viewer. He adjusted the tripod and squinted into the viewer again clearly focusing the camera on Grayson. He again focused the lens on the others in the room and quickly pressing the "On" and "Off" buttons recorded those present. He again pressed the "On" button and returned to his seat.

"Mr. Grayson," said Hewitt, "your attorney tells us that you are ready to make a statement concerning the Baby Franco investigation."

"I am," said Grayson.

"And your attorney is present," said Hewitt.

"Yes," said Grayson. "Ralph Fitzmorris, my attorney, is here."

"Counselor," said Hewitt, would you mind identifying yourself for the record."

"I am Ralph Fitzmorris," said Grayson's attorney. "I represent Mr. Grayson and I will advise him during the course of this statement."

"For the record, Mr. Grayson," said Hewitt, "please state your name and address."

Grayson took a sip of the overcooked coffee before him and looked around the room. "My name is Avery Grayson. I live at 1203 Garden Street, Honesdale. I own and operate a funeral service at that same location. I live on the second floor."

There was a knock at the door.

Hewitt opened the door. Fitzmorris could see Wayne County Prosecutor Henry Silva standing outside the door, whispering to Hewitt.

"Excuse me for a moment," said Hewitt, closing the door behind him.

Grayson shot Fitzmorris a worried look. Fitzmorris placed his hand on Grayson's arm.

"Try to relax, Avery."

150

Three minutes later Detective Hewitt returned to the room with Henry Silva.

"Avery," said Hewitt, "Judge Collins has signed a court order for the exhumation of Gregory Bedford, an infant who died at the age of 8 months. This infant was under the care of Dr. Nichols, who paid for the funeral arrangements, which you handled. Based on the results of that exhumation we also expect to exhume the bodies of Baby Caroline Whittier and Baby Michael Jennings, also infants under the care of Dr. Nichols. He paid for the funeral arrangements that you handled. I wanted you and your attorney to have this information, Avery, before you began your statement. Now, do you still wish to make a statement to us at this time?"

"Gentlemen," said Fitzmorris, loud enough to be heard over the whimpering of Avery Grayson, who had placed his head on his arms on the table like a kindergarten student at rest time. "I'd like a few minutes to confer with my client--alone, if I may."

"You've got ten minutes, Mr. Fitzmorris," said Silva.

"Thank you," said Fitzmorris as Hewitt, the stenographer, and Silva left the room. Hewitt neglected to turn off the video recorder as he left the room. When the door closed Fitzmorris addressed the sobbing Grayson. "It's time to make the best deal we can, Avery. Based on what you've told me, you still have some leverage left, but you'll have to give up Dr. Nichols. You can't hold anything back."

"That damm Nichols," sobbed Grayson. "He did this to me."

****

The following morning a sparse cemetery crew assembled at the grave of Gregory Bedford. The infant burial section of the cemetery was lined with poplar trees whose early summer pollen balls filled the enclosure with white puffs of "heavenly clouds, the type angels sit on when they come to take a child's soul to heaven" as the designers of the Children's Garden so aptly put it. The crew foreman examined the paperwork one last time before he gave the order to the driver of the green John Deere Utility Tractor to commence the excavation. "Careful," he needlessly added as the teeth of the shovel scratched the earth. The removed bronze grave marker sat to the left of the grave. Like the precise cut of the skilled surgeon the three-foot wide shovel scooped and emptied the hallowed dirt onto a utility wagon nearby. Presently the shovel tugged at an obstacle – the roots of one of the poplar trees had encircled the vault as if to keep the child in the grip of eternal rest. Several workers grabbing lopping shears snipped and cut the roots as the shovel applied upward pressure on the cement vault. Slowly the vault was lifted several inches as a worker placed a steel cable under it. The ends of the cable were looped around the shovel and it slowly lifted the vault from the ground. As the vault cleared the grave, an office employee standing nearby shed a tear. She would always remember her thoughts that day. She was reminded of the gospel song, "I will raise you up on the last day" as she watched. A grounds crew employee guided the vault onto a small flatbed trailer that was backing to the gravesite. The vault containing the casket of baby Gregory was slowly lowered and securely tied to the wooden bed. A piece of plywood was placed over the opened grave and several orange traffic cones encircled it. The truck pulled away as the men talked about what just happened. No one ever recalled the exhumation of a child. It was no surprise later that day when the empty casket of Gregory Bedford was opened at the medical examiner's lab. Later that day Judge Collins authorized the exhumation of baby's Whittier and Jennings. The results were the same – empty coffins.

Several days later, baby Gregory's casket was returned to the grave. The same cemetery crew was on hand to conduct the burial. Grace Bedford was there as was Fr. Maloney from nearby St. Athanasius parish. Several of Grace's friends were there to console and support her. Unbeknownst to her friends, the casket was empty. Fr. Maloney conducted the second burial rite for the child in absentia. "A religious formality," he instructed. The crew foreman told Grace that he had told his young daughter about Gregory and his daughter gave him a stuffed animal to place in the vault with Gregory in case he wanted "Chester the Magic Pony" to play with. Grace wept and thanked the foreman for his kindness.

CHAPTER 11

Diane Huffman, Judge Collins's secretary, interrupted a pre-trial conference on the next case on the judge's docket.

"Sorry to interrupt, Judge. Grace Bedford is here. She wants to know if you have a few minutes to see her."

"Grace Bedford," said the judge. "Yes, by all means. Just give us a couple of minutes to finish up here and I'll be right with her. Make her comfortable, will you Diane? Now then, gentlemen," he said, turning his attention once again to the two attorneys before him, "unless either of you has anything else to bring up..."

"No, that about does it, Your Honor," said the assistant prosecutor.

"We've touched on everything, Judge," added the public defender.

"OK, then," said the judge. "Yours is the first case out of the box on Monday. You'll both be ready to go, your witnesses will be available, am I correct? Good. Then I won't be hearing any motions for a continuance from either of you, right?"

"The state is ready to go."

"As is the defense."

"Well, looks like we're done here, gentlemen," said the judge. "And I have another matter to attend to." The visitors cleared the room as the judge ran his hand through his hair. He thought of his daughter and experienced a rush of painful nostalgia. He arose from his desk and walked to his outer office. He realized the walk to his door felt like an hour of heavy work-out. He wondered who he would see when he opened it.

Dressed in a tan blouse and dark blue pants, Grace appeared to be the epitome of style and culture. Pearls accented the blouse and her dark brown hair was gathered in pony tail fashion. She wasn't the doughty person Collins expected to see but exuded an air of calm and refinement.

"Mrs. Bedford," said the judge, walking to the woman who had risen from a chair in the outer office. "Thank you so much for stopping by. I had intended to call you yesterday, I'm sorry..."

"No need to apologize, Judge. I appreciate your willingness to see me." She extended her hand and firmly grasped Collins's hand as she spoke.

"I am happy to do so, Mrs. Bedford. Won't you please join me in chambers?" Pausing at the door he turned back to his secretary. "Diane, please hold all my calls and would you get us two waters? I hope that's OK Mrs. Bedford," he added glancing at her. "I'm fine, Judge, but by all means get one for yourself." He mouthed "never mind" to Diane as he closed the door to his chambers and walked to his desk.

"Please sit down, Mrs. Bedford," he said. "I want you to know that I appreciate what you have done. I know it wasn't easy for you."

"Well, Your Honor, that's why I stopped in. I was hoping that you could tell me what they found out about my Gregory. The police won't tell me anything. It's all so secretive. So I thought you might help me. What happened?"

"You mean no one has contacted you?

"No, Judge, No one."

"This is unforgivable. Let me make a phone call right now," Collins said, obviously irritated. He picked up the phone and turned away from Mrs. Bedford as he spoke.

"Diane, please get me Henry Silva on the line. If he isn't in, tell them to put me through to wherever he is. I want to speak with him now."

The judge turned back toward the young woman, saying, "I am ashamed and embarrassed, that no one contacted you. I should have made the arrangements myself." The phone extension rang. "Excuse me."

He turned away again. "Yes, Henry, this is Collins. Never mind how I am, this is not a social call. I have Mrs. Bedford in my office. Yes, she's here right now. Henry, she tells me no one has contacted her about the investigation. Is that correct?"

There was a brief pause before Collins, now openly angry, responded. "Security and confidentially be damned, Henry. Without this woman's help your investigation was going nowhere fast. Did you want her to hear about it on the news or have some reporter call her? Leaks happen. It's just dumb luck that this story hasn't hit the papers." The judge paused as the prosecutor responded. "Henry, in this matter I don't care about the letter of the law. I'd prefer a little sensitivity and compassion, and if you can't manage that, how about a modicum of common sense or basic decency." He glanced at Grace and continued the call. "Yes, that's right. I do intend to tell her because I trust her, and because we owe her that much. If you don't like it, you could seek a gag order against me…I didn't think so. Yes, I am going to talk to her now. I'll call you later."

Collins jammed the receiver onto the desk phone and turned to face Mrs. Bedford once again.

"I'm sorry, Judge, I didn't mean to get anyone in trouble," she said.

"No one is in trouble, Mrs. Bedford. Henry and I go back a long way. We are good friends," he smiled. "He lets me have it but good when I deserve it."

"Is the news about my Gregory so terrible?"

"It is disturbing."

"Judge, I've lived through my son's death. Whatever this is, it can't be as bad as that. Just go ahead and tell me. I think I can stand anything now."

Collins recalled who his own daughter must have felt when her son died. Could this be any more heart wrenching, he thought. His mind rushed through a thousand ways to begin to tell her. But the more he thought about the best way the more his mind stammered. "Just say it," came into his mind.

"Well, there is no way to ease into this. Mrs. Bedford, your son's coffin was empty."

Grace looked uncomprehendingly at the judge and blinked.

"According to the lab," continued the judge, "your son was never buried in that grave."

She gasped and held her hand to her mouth. Tears readily rolled down her cheeks.

"I'm sorry, Judge, I don't understand."

"I don't either. But the fact is nobody was ever placed in that coffin. There were no signs of burial, no evidence of any DNA whatsoever." He paused and wondered whether the direct approach was the best. It was.

"Then where is...who would...why would someone do this? What possible reason? The funeral home..."

"I do not know. The police have some theories and some suspects..."

"What are they, what do they think happened? Do they know what happened to my Gregory? Where is he? How could anyone do this to him? Oh, my God," she shouted!

"I understand how upsetting this is..."

"Upsetting, where's my little boy," she pleaded.

"Yes, yes. As far as I know," said the judge, "they aren't certain who took Gregory's body or why."

"Crazy people, that's who took him! But, but they have some ideas, some theories, you said. Suspects," she said as she began to calm herself wanting to learn the truth.

"Since we spoke I realize I also have a personal interest in your son. We are distant but kindred spirits, sort of to say. So although there is nothing conclusive at this time,

Mrs. Bedford, as soon as I learn something concrete, I will let you know."

"Oh my God," said Mrs. Bedford more out of relief than a prayer.

"I wish there was something more I could do for you," said Collins as he began to feel helpless. In all his years as a judge, there were fewer more difficult times finding the right word of encouragement than now. So, he fell back on the good hostess rejoinder. "Are you sure you wouldn't like a glass of water? Coffee?"

"No, Judge. Nothing. My God, I don't know what to think. I'm, I'm stunned. Who are the suspects? Tell me Judge, you said yourself, I have a right to know."

"Mrs. Bedford, please. Strictly speaking I shouldn't have told you as much as I have. I think you deserve to know the basic information the police have concerning your son. During the course of an investigation the police consider all sorts of possibilities and theories. Most come to nothing. It would be better if you waited for more solid information. I don't want you filling your heart and mind with 'supposes' or 'maybes' or 'what ifs'. I will personally see to it that you are advised about future developments relating to your son."

"I'm sorry, Judge. You have been very kind. I knew you would be helpful. When you called me that first time...you told me about your grandson...I knew... you'd... understand. Oh, damn." She hurriedly reached for her pocketbook and removed a handkerchief. "I promised myself this wouldn't happen again," she said through her tears. "I thought I was stronger than this."

"You're one of the strongest people I've ever met," said Collins. "You go ahead and cry. Take your time." He felt inadequate as he gave her permission to be herself.

"All the tears, they change nothing. Nothing. It's so pointless."

"Yes, I know. The tears, the prayers, the anger, the grief. None of it seems to help."

"I keep searching for a reason, a purpose. That's why, when you called, I said yes. Because you told me it might help someone. Gregory's death, his life, sometimes it seems so pointless."

"I know. And the pain, the grief, it is like being ill. Helpless, lost. There is no way to improve the situation, no compromises to be made, and no way to make anything better. When my grandson died, my daughter was in so much pain, I felt--for the first time in my adult life--absolutely powerless. I fought against myself for consolation. But that moment would take years to achieve."

"Yes, powerless and insignificant," said Grace. "My entire world became, well, like it was transparent, not solid. Like cellophane. It was like my soul, not me, my soul was screaming in pain and my mind switched off. For a while I lost any real awareness of my own body, of my physical needs. I don't remember eating or sleeping, or dressing, or bathing. I must have, there were people around me, but it was like I was sleepwalking. I was both present to others and not there at the same time. Unconscious, an emotional stupor."

"Yes," said the Judge, "I experienced something very much like that. And then, for me, that was the point when I realized that despite everything, I was still here. And immediately on the heels of that thought, it may have been simultaneous with that thought, came the realization that I didn't have to be…that I was finite."

Mrs. Bedford had stopped crying and was looking directly at the judge. "Yes, Judge. That moment when you equate life with pain. You believe life, consciousness, is all pain. Not joy and pain, not sadness or boredom or anticipation, just unrelenting deadening pain. From that vantage point death, oblivion, looks good. I was there. Like being on the edge of a cliff…"

"…And nothing in front of you but blackness. A bottomless pit. Oblivion," said the judge.

"Yes. And everything becomes simple. In that moment your life is reduced to two options," said the young woman, excited to find someone who understood. "Take that one step forward into oblivion. It would be so easy, one little step and the pain is gone, the world ends and you're never again alone with your inescapable misery. Or you can turn away from the edge of oblivion..."

"And find your way back," said the judge.

"Yes, you can choose to live, Judge. You can't have the same life, but you can live. It does change you, doesn't it, the grief? Because I'm not the same person I was before I was on the edge of that cliff. When you turn away from that self-pity and misery, you really turn to others. Having suffered that pain, knowing that too few prayers are answered the way that we want them answered, I want to help others avoid that pain. I want to be the answer to someone's prayer."

"Yes, it changes us," said the judge. "I'm not saying what happened was worth the change. I'd never say that. I'd give up everything I have to return the world to the way it was before. Everything..." Judge Collins paused, and turned his chair away from Grace Bedford. He removed his glasses and absent-mindedly cleaned the lenses. He turned back toward Grace when she began speaking again.

"I was never really in favor of ending Gregory's treatment, you know? I wasn't sure. But Greg, my ex-husband, he was absolutely sure. When I look back on it now, it seems to me that he was relieved. But I recall the British novelist's word...the past is a foreign country, they do things different there. Although I don't believe I'm rewriting my life I have to think that maybe this was his way out of the mess? Greg wasn't ready to be a father. Hell, he wasn't even ready to be a faithful husband. Everything I cherished and loved was taken from me. When the baby first got sick, Greg and I leaned on each other. But the accusations and the blame started as soon as they told us how sick little Gregory was. Greg Sr. thought it was my fault. I should have taken more vitamins, even doubled the pre-natal prescription, exercised more, and drank more milk, a hundred little things that might have helped our baby to be healthier. Our friends tried to help us. But the marriage ended when we decided to let Gregory die. Maybe I'm being unfair to my ex-husband. This may be my way of absolving myself from guilt. He was sure. I wasn't. Maybe I would have agreed with him eventually."

"An awful decision for anyone to have to make," said the judge.

"Greg was so sick, and in terrible pain," said Mrs. Bedford. "I may have gotten to the same point as my husband. The fact is we both signed the authorization to discontinue treatment to let nature take its course without heroic medical intervention. I may say I wasn't ready to do it, but I did it. I can tell you one thing, Judge."

"What's that?"

"I don't think I would make the same choice today. If they could assure me that the pain could be controlled, I know I wouldn't. I'd take him home, take care of him and cherish the time we'd have. That's what I don't have, Judge. Memories of me caring for him. I hardly ever got to hold my own baby. They said just my holding him caused him pain. How can a mother holding her child create anything but life for both? He was in ICU almost the entire time. We signed the papers, and he was dead 36 hours later. I wasn't even with him when he died. Everyone said it would be best if I wasn't there. I was enough of a coward to follow their advice. I'd do it differently today, but life doesn't give you second chances."

"Seldom," said Judge Collins. "All too seldom."

"Tell me about your daughter, Judge. I'd like to meet her sometime."

"That's impossible. She died."

"Forgive me, Judge, I didn't know."

"You remind me of her," said the judge. "You even have the same color hair. She wore hers a bit shorter than you, but still, there's a resemblance. Eric was our first grandchild, you know. Emily was an only child, so that door has closed. No grandchildren. Beth--that's my wife--and I went out to Denver when Eric was born. Stayed the whole month. Made the assignment judge sputter a bit, but I did it.

"He was a beautiful, happy child. Here, I have some pictures," said the judge, reaching for his wallet. He removed several photos and handed them to Mrs. Bedford.

"Look at that smile," said Mrs. Bedford. "And your daughter looks so happy too."

"Yes, she was radiant. She really was. I had never seen her happier. You know, that picture was taken on the day Beth and I left Denver to return home. It may be the last time I saw my daughter smile. She was the one who found Eric, you know, in the morning. Four months and six days old. She never really recovered."

"It must have been an awful shock."

"It tore the marriage apart. But in fairness to Jerry, her husband, I think it was Emily's drinking as much as anything else. It was an impossible situation for him to deal with. Her drinking prevented him from being able to comfort her and it prevented her from helping him deal with his grief. She drove him away, really."

"How sad."

"Yes. Beth and I went back for Eric's funeral. Our own grief blinded us to the extent of the drinking problem. Emily would have a few drinks during the day and every night she'd say that she needed a few more to help her sleep. Claimed she couldn't sleep without it. I even poured her a few nightcaps. Who'd begrudge anyone a shot or two under those circumstances? Six months later she was dead. Car accident. Drunk. Thank God she didn't take anyone else with her. She stood on the edge of that cliff and embraced the abyss. Perhaps if she had your strength she might have survived."

"I had time to adjust, to prepare. I knew my baby was going to die. I even knew when. Your daughter had no warning. None."

"Grace...ah, do you mind if I call you Grace?"

"Not at all. But please don't be insulted if I continue to call you 'Judge'. I wouldn't feel comfortable calling you anything else."

"Not at all, Grace. I've been a judge so long; all my friends call me 'Judge'. Now, I was about to tell you that you are a very wise and compassionate young woman. I have not spoken so frankly about my daughter and Eric with anyone else. It's comforting, but unfortunate, Grace, to know that someone has been through the same emotional turmoil. It doesn't change anything, but it was good to talk about. Feel like I've excised a few demons. Unburdened myself. I thank you."

"And thank you for telling me what you could about my son. I know now that you will tell me more as soon as you can."

"You've got my word. In fact, after you leave here today, I will instruct the prosecutor's office to contact you before they make any public statements on this case and before they make any arrests."

"You can do that?"

"I'm a judge. I can do anything but change the past."

****

As Grace Bedford was leaving Collins's chambers, Detective Hewitt was walking into Wallington's office with a cardboard banker's box full of files.

"What you got there, Dan?" said the chief. "Doing some housecleaning?"

"In a way, Chief. These are the Baby Franco files. I'm ready to arrest Dr. Nichols on a charge of kidnapping. I wanted to go over the information with you before bringing it all to Prosecutor Silva."

"You afraid he's going leave the area? Are you thinking he's a flight risk?" asked the chief.

"Not really, but there's no need to sit on all this information," said Hewitt. "I don't know how close Grayson and Nichols are. Grayson may warn Nichols. If he does, Nichols may decide to take a vacation to some locale that doesn't believe in extradition."

"He doesn't strike me as a runner," said Wallington.

"Probably not, but still, we gain nothing by waiting. We've got more than enough to bring him in. Why wait?"

"May I point out," said Chief Wallington, "Dr. Nichols insists that Avery Grayson was the last person to have the bodies."

"Like he'd have no reason to lie about a thing like that. What the hell, we can hit Grayson with several charges as well. The prosecutor's deal with him is no jail time if he continues to give us his full cooperation. We never said he wouldn't face charges. We can charge them both with conspiracy..."

"Nichols is a well-respected member of this community. He has a lot of friends and supporters," said Wallington.

"He's popular. Doesn't mean he's innocent."

"That's Henry's call," said Wallington. "Sometimes these lawyers want us to do all their work for them. They aren't satisfied unless we get a confession and a videotape of the perpetrator committing the crime."

"You don't think Henry will OK this arrest?"

"Don't know. He's a little gun shy since the judge jumped in his shit about our not contacting that Bedford woman. He may want something more solid. What about the license plate angle?"

"You mean the partial number Grayson says he saw at the hospital the night he pretended to pick up Baby Franco?"

"You know damn well that's the one," said Wallington, "and I know damn well by your answer that you haven't run that down yet. Did you even request the state police computer check?"

"Yeah, I requested it. They gave me a report."

"And...?"

"Nothing yet, Chief."

"Nothing? Does that mean it's a dead end or that you haven't gotten off your dead end to run down the list of plates?"

"You know all he gave us was a partial plate, 'I J', that's all he remembers, the plate began with an 'I' and a 'J'. You know how many registered vehicles there are in this state?"

"Can't recall the question every coming up in all my years of police work detective. Enlighten me?"

"North of 8 million."

"That would explain all the traffic..."

"Do you know how many of those 8 million plates begin with 'I J'?"

"You have the advantage on me again Detective..."

"I've got a list of better than 7,000 plates beginning with an 'I' and a 'J'. That's just those beginning with 'I J'."

The chief let out an appreciative whistle. "Welcome to the glamorous world of modern day police work, wallowing through miles of computer print outs."

"It will take me weeks, months to run down that many plates. Let's nab Nichols now, and then I can do the legwork on the plates."

"It's Henry's call, so let's call Henry," said the chief. "But don't be surprised if he wants you to nail down that license plate angle before we collar the good doctor."

"Bet you a beer that Silva says pick him up," said Hewitt. "He wants to put a lid on this case as much as I do."

Hewitt lost the bet. Silva wanted Hewitt to track down the license plates. Silva had also decided he would ask Judge Collins for a wiretap on Dr. Nichols.

"The tap might reveal where he sent Baby Franco," argued Silva. "That's worth a few days wait. Use that time to get started on the license plate lead."

"You're the boss, Mr. Prosecutor," said Hewitt. "I do have one hunch I want to check out."

"What hunch?"

"I started with vanity plates, shorter list, you know. And one is kind of interesting."

"What is it?" asked the prosecutor.

"A bible reference. I JHN5-2. I, the Roman numeral one; JHN for John; five for chapter five and two for verse two. I John, Chapter 5, Verse 2."

"OK, it's a bible verse," said Silva.

"Yeah, but if my hunch is right, it's like a bumper sticker for what's going on here."

"So what's the verse say?"

"I've got the files with me, hold on a second. Checked the internet translation. Here it is. *We can be sure that we love God's children if we love God himself and do what he has commanded us.*' See? It fits."

"Sure it does. Just like a hundred other bible passages would fit. But listen, I don't care where you start with the list, you're the detective. Just get on it. I'll see if I can get in to see the judge tomorrow morning."

"Well, I guess I'm going for a ride tomorrow. The bible plate car is registered to a couple in southern Lancaster County."

"Your call, Detective. I'll let the chief know what Judge Collins decides."

****

It was shortly after 4:30 p.m. that same day when Dr. Nichols called Philip Duran's Philadelphia office from a recently purchased Wal-Mart phone.

Duran didn't recognize the phone number. He could only guess who the caller was. He followed his instincts. "Fred?" asked Duran .

"Yes. Can you talk?"

"I'll close the door. This is unexpected. What's going on"

"A lot's been happening around here. Looks like I'll need a lawyer. A good one."

"What's happened?" asked Duran.

"Grayson broke ranks. Made a deal. Told them everything he knows."

Duran flinched. "That's quite a statement. How do you know?"

"He called me. Can you believe it? He tells the police everything he knows and then calls me like that makes it OK. Said he felt guilty about turning me in. My fault for involving him in the first place. He was a weak man. No commitment to the network. Only needed money. That's why he cooperated with us and that's why he talked. The disturbing thing is that he said they knew about the others, the other children. They knew!" said Nichols.

"If he's told them about the others; this could threaten the entire network." He reflected then added, "I'll get you our attorney but first I should inform the 'Boss'."

"You know, Phil, I've never met the 'Boss'".

"Long ago, when we started, there were three of us. We decided that for the safety of everyone and to insure maximum success that we would compartmentalize the network. It was an easy decision who would be the 'capo di tutti capi', the overall boss. That was easy thanks to his lottery winnings. We can pray and hope and trust and believe, but without a lot of money, nothing happens. Even

St. Paul had benefactors along the way. We have ours. But I've said too much. Ignore that last comment. My role was to manage the finances and Evelyn was chosen to analyze the medical data necessary to create the safe havens that were needed, and manage the volunteers. Evelyn was a rehabilitation nurse. Her knowledge of handicapping conditions fit perfectly to designing safe havens on an individualized basis to suit the children's needs. She ordered the supplies and solicited volunteers. The boss paid the bills and I over saw all legal and financial matters. Evelyn was the best. But as heaven would have it, she developed breast cancer. It was quick. Eventually that left me and the Boss. I've picked up the volunteer end. The Boss picked up the medical end."

"I see. So there were three, I didn't know that. Evelyn enlisted me. I knew about her and her passion for life's issues. And then she, well sort of, handed me off to you for hospital selection and hospital transference, background, and credential issues. I should have known but didn't question the medical angle," Nichols confessed. "Will I ever meet him, you called the Boss a 'he'?"

"Maybe one day…formally. He'll contact you. But for everyone's safety let's remain cautious, OK?"

"So the boss is male. Good to know."

"Enough for now, Fred. Let's talk about our current dilemma."

"This must stop with me. It can't go up the chain of command."

"Why do you say that?"

"Grayson knows one thing. He didn't receive those bodies. He doesn't know who received them, what happened to them. He doesn't even know if the infants were dead or alive. I'm the only one the police know of who has any of that information and I'm not talking."

"You'll be disgraced, hated. They'll go for a prison term, and that could get ugly," said Duran. "Are you prepared for that?"

"'Blessed are those who are persecuted in the cause of right: theirs is the kingdom of heaven.' To be arrested for doing God's will puts me in the best of company. I pray I'm worthy of the honor. My future is secondary to the safety of the network."

"I know that, Fred. I know all about you, thanks to Evelyn. But, really, how are you holding up?" said Duran.

"Truthfully, I've been better. But before we go any further, I want you to know that there is nothing, nothing they can do to me that would make me talk. I went into this with my eyes wide open. I always knew that one day it could come to this. I am prepared to do whatever is necessary to protect the network."

"We appreciate that, Doctor. But let's see what we can do to extract you from this dilemma and preserve the network. I'll be asking Jim Fallon to go to Honesdale immediately. Do you know Jim?"

"Fallon? The one who's on Fox News all the time?"

"Yes, he has made quite a name for himself within the movement, and within the ACLU, although they don't seem to be as fond of him as we are," said Duran. "He is the best lawyer I know, and, more importantly, a man with absolutely unshakable faith. The Boss mentioned that we make him the 'third man'. He has been a member of the network longer than you have. You can disclose everything to him with absolute confidence. If there's a way out of this Jim will find it, don't you worry."

"I'm not, Phil."

"Fred, the network takes care of its own. You have been involved in nearly a dozen resurrections. We won't turn our backs on you."

"Thank you, Phil," said the doctor.

"Our prayers are with you, Doctor," said Philip Duran. "Jim will call you directly."

"Won't it be suspicious that I'm represented by a nationally prominent attorney?

"Not at all. It is only natural that a prominent pro-life attorney would contact a prominent pro-life doctor who has a legal problem."

"What about payment?"

"Money is the easy part. You'll pay Jim's usual legal fees directly from your account. All perfectly normal. If you're not liquid, mortgage the house. Later, we can arrange for one of our affiliate groups to buy the house and make a present of it to you. Because of your public stand on pro-life issues, raising money for your defense will be no problem. We'll have friends establish a defense fund. Nothing will be traced back to the network."

"I guess my real concern is the publicity," said Nichols. "They are going to paint me as some kind of fiend. What did I do with the bodies? The speculation has been gruesome. To admit the truth would jeopardize the entire Resurrection Network. The opposition will enjoy equating my pro-life stance with my newly earned status as some sort of monster. I don't care what lies they spread about me, but they'll try to smear the entire movement with the same brush. Serious harm could be done, just as the abortion clinic bombings and shootings did some time ago."

"That is a problem," said Duran. "However, if you, Jim, and I can't figure a way out, we'll just offer it up to the Lord. He'll lead us out of this desert."

"Amen," said Dr. Nichols.

"The Lord be with you, Doctor," said Philip Duran. Then he paused and added, "How do you feel about the great northwest, Fred?"

"I hear it rains quite a bit there, Phil."

"OK, then. May God be with us all," said Nichols, hanging up the phone.

Philip Duran immediately called Jim Fallon. A Penn Law graduate, Fallon, like Nichols, was a bachelor. His leisure hours were spent attracting new business clients while attending social affairs in the trendier parts of Philadelphia and the Main Line. He met Vivian Modell on several occasions and correctly sized her up as "Venus with brains and money." He noted to Duran that she could be 'dangerous' if goaded or threatened. Duran decided not to share that assessment with Doug Fedderson.

After breaching Fallon's pleasant secretary's "Do not disturb" telephone de rigueur response, he finally got through to Fallon. Without any customary cordiality Duran simply blurted, "We need you to get to Honesdale."

"Honesdale."

"The situation is deteriorating. Grayson is cooperating with the police. Nichols claims that Grayson told him that he had given a statement about all four Honesdale resurrections. Nichols expects to be arrested soon. He's been with us for years. Very loyal, very effective. Believes he won't crack, but if he does, or if they link us to Grayson, the entire network could be compromised. Fedderson's also been keeping me advised throughout. He's worried about Nichols. Calls him a 'worthy soldier'."

"I understand. I've been keeping an eye on the situation," said Fallon. "It has always played out more 'chancy' than the others. Any chance we could buy our way out of this?"

"That's what you'll have to judge, Jim. It's probably too late for Grayson, but you should complete that package anyway. Raise the ante by another $1 million. I doubt that he'd take the money at this point, but our additional generosity will cause him to resent the deal he got from the state. Not being able to get his hands on that money will eat away at him, and he'll blame the state. The less willing he is to cooperate, the better it is for us. And who knows, there is always the possibility he'll decide to take the money."

"What about this detective, what's his name, Hewitt. Can he be bought? Who else might be persuaded to see the light? Damn, I hate this part of the business. Tampering, bribery, accessory to the fact, after the fact and the list goes on."

"Fedderson says to stay away from Hewitt. Other possible players might include the biological father and his attorney, although they don't seem to be much of a factor now. Even if they were, I think we could get them out of the way for less than $100,000. After that we're talking about touching prosecutors and judges, big money and big risks. You'll have to decide how to proceed, but it appears to me the quicker Nichols disappears, the better it is for the network. And by the way, the biological mother shows unbelievable signs of improvement. She's walking the hospital halls! Becoming a real hospital socialite. That's another one of our concerns that we didn't plan for. But for now, let's focus on the attorney, the biological father, and Fred Nichols."

"And if Nichols doesn't agree with the plan?"

"We've spoken about relocation. He's aboard."

"Understood. Let's hope he'll like, ah, where did you say he's headed?"

"I'm still looking."

"Good. I'll leave for Honesdale first thing tomorrow."

"I told Nichols you'd call him tonight."

"That's my next call."

The next morning Jim Fallon left his home in Greenwich, Connecticut, on a three-hour drive to Honesdale and coincidentally at the same time, Detective Hewitt began his three-hour drive from Honesdale to Lancaster County. As Fallon approached the New York-Pennsylvania line, he decided to call Dr. Nichols to inform him that he would be arriving at the doctor's hospital office by 12:30 p.m. and to advise Nichols that his office and home phone might be tapped. "In fact," he added, "this call might be recorded."

"If the police have erred and targeted you as a suspect," said Fallon, playing to his assumed audience, "you have to act as if every phone was tapped and that your office is bugged. The police have the ability to see criminal intent in the most harmless conversations."

Fallon was partially right. Prosecutor Silva was in Judge Collins's chambers seeking a court-ordered wiretap. But the Judge Collins was not cooperating.

"This would be a big, big mistake, Henry," said the judge. "Too many lines…a house, office phone and he can use practically any phone in the hospital. What are you going to do? Tap all the hospital lines? You can't tap enough of the phones he can use to be effective and you expose yourself to a public outcry about doctor patient-privilege, and what about some sticky family privacy issues. What, if in the process of gathering evidence for your case you inadvertently overhear and record a family scandal, or record plans for an illicit rendezvous? You don't need the wiretap to make your case. Henry, you're lucky I'm here to save you from these public relations blunders."

"I'm just an ingrate, I guess," said Silva. "I don't feel thankful at all."

"So, how's the investigation going outside of my lack of cooperation?"

"Hey, the investigation is continuing. Hewitt's on his way to Lancaster County today, tracking down a partial PA Department of Motor Vehicles registration."

"How's that fit in?"

"Grayson gave it to us. Says there was a car with a vanity license that began with an 'I' and a 'J'."

"I and J?"

"Yes, the Roman numeral I and the letter J. One J something something something. He's checking out what he thinks is a promising lead today."

"What makes one more promising than another?"

173

"Hewitt thinks it's a vanity plate that has some religious significance, I JHN 5-2."

"That's religious, huh?"

"That's Hewitt's hunch. A bible verse, I John, Chapter 5, verse 2, it fits in with the case."

"I'm not as familiar with my bible as I should be, Henry. What's that verse say?"

"Hewitt checked it and told me. It's something like: 'We love God's children if we do what God commands'. That's a paraphrase. But you get the idea."

"So the license plate is used as a what, a way to convert people?"

"Who knows, Judge? Some people feel they have to take every opportunity to proselytize. Remember that guy with that rainbow colored fright wig that used to be on TV all the time at sporting events? He'd be at all the big time televised sporting events, NBA playoffs, World Series, championship boxing. All the big games and his seat always faced the TV cameras."

"I remember him," said the judge. "He would act all herky-jerky and hold up a big sign referring to some bible verse. I haven't seen him lately. Was there only one guy or was it some sort of evangelical franchise where believers could get great seats if they agreed to dress weird and wave bible placards. Can't help but wonder where'd the money for those great tickets come from?"

"I don't know, Judge. It was amazing how often he'd pop up. Imagine getting tickets to the World Series and ending up sitting behind that guy? I'd go ballistic!"

"You have an innate, if somewhat perverse, sense of justice, Henry," said the judge. "So, Hewitt's off tracking down a religious license plate."

"Yes," said Silva. "But since you won't give us the wiretap, I've decided that even if this 'I John' license plate thing is a dead end, I'll have Hewitt bring Dr. Nichols in tomorrow."

"What's the charge going to be?"

"Kidnapping."

"Henry, I don't have the case law at my fingertips, but I don't think you can kidnap a dead body."

"Judge, we don't think the infants were dead when they were kidnapped."

"What do you mean?"

"Hewitt's theory and I think he may be right, is that Dr. Nichols forged the death certificates and arranged for phony funerals as a cover-up for removing the infants from the hospital and taking them someplace else where they could be cared for, or God forbid, carved up."

"Why on earth..."

"It was Dr. Nichols's way of avoiding having to discontinue treatment for the infants. In each case the parents had decided to modify or withdraw treatment and let the infants die a prematurely but natural death. He sees that as a morally unacceptable."

"You mean if the parents or the guardians, or no one person, in the case of the Franco baby had yet not decided to modify treatment, Nichols took it on himself to fake the baby's death and proceed with a phony funeral and care for the child elsewhere?"

"That's what we think, Judge."

Collins paused then took a deep disbelieving breath. "That's incredible. Kidnapping to save lives, no ransom except life itself."

"I don't know about saving lives, Judge. That's a medical decision. But, each of these kids was terminally ill. It was only a matter of time. The parents, the guardians, whoever, were all convinced that treatment only prolonged the child's suffering…"

"And yes, I recall that once the guardian makes an informed legal life altering decision, no one has a right to interfere…New Jersey Supreme Court 1976, in the matter of Karen Quinlan, an alleged incompetent, case law, period, done." He reflected. "I always had a problem with that decision. It was a difficult and a painful judgment that I thought someone might want to reconsider at some future date."

Hewitt looked at him quizzically and wondered to himself, "What did he just say? He disagrees with that decades old bedrock decision?" He added, "I can't imagine a more difficult decision, Judge. And that is why I find it outrageous that someone would interject themselves in such a private matter and contravene the parents' wishes."

"So there is a possibility some of these children might still be alive?"

"I suppose it's possible."

"Incredible."

"Here's an interesting legal point. Say one of the critically ill children died while being transported from the hospital to wherever it is he decided to send them. I think that would support a murder charge against Dr. Nichols."

"If you could prove the cause of death was related to the unauthorized removal of the infant from the hospital and the medical care provided therein."

"But what if there was no medical care *per se* provided by the hospital?" he quizzed.

"Now you are sounding more like a lawyer than a detective. But to your original question…death while being kidnapped…

"Yes, while being transported."

"The law would support that charge, Henry. But you know as well as I that a halfway decent defense attorney could win that case on emotion alone. I could write the defense summation now: 'Ladies and gentlemen of the jury, the parents of this child decided it was his time to die. The hospital, the nurses, the doctors all decided that it was his time to die. All save one! Doctor Nichols chose life! He fought to save this child's life. How is it that the only person who was willing to risk everything to save this child's life

176

stands before you accused of murder? Is this justice? Ladies and gentleman of the jury, I ask each of you, 'How far would you go to save a life'? How you going to win a case like that?"

"It would be a challenge, Judge. You know, that wiretap might give us the location of those infants. Care to reconsider?"

Collins' mind ran the gamut from praise for Nichols to understanding the intent of the law. Heroism versus the rights of the parent. Virtue versus fear of pain. Courage versus just plain fear...the parental fear of the future, fear of losing one's level of comfort to live one's life for the sake of another. Were all this merely a question of parental comfort and lack of trust in a merciful God? Why was it OK to accept God's good gifts and anathema to even consider those moments we call 'wrong'? Our own personal calling is sacrifice for others, in self-giving to those we love or don't love according to the Bible. He felt an awakened legal conscience and he welcomed it.

"Nah, your guy is too smart to be phoning some kind of children's halfway house at this time. And if he was reckless enough to make a call from a home or office line in the past you'll find out when you subpoena the phone records."

"Had to ask, Judge, thanks for hearing me out."

"And thank you, Henry, for the background information on this remarkable case. Takes me back to my days as a prosecutor. You must be very excited."

"This is a unique one, that's for sure. Tell me, do you ever miss it, being a prosecutor. Piecing together a case, bringing it all together?"

"Once in a while I get the urge to get in on an investigation again. But then I think of how much less stressful it is to be the one who can grant the wiretap order than it is to be the one who needs the wiretap order. Being a judge has its rewards."

"Well, Judge, I'll be going."

"Enjoyed talking with you, Henry.

"Me too, Judge," said Silva leaving the judge's chambers.

Collins consulted his Rolodex, an antiquated but reliable system, and thumbed for a name and dialed a number.

"State Police Barracks," came the answer on the other line.

"Yes, this is Judge Everett Collins from Honesdale, Wayne County. I'd like to speak with Lieutenant Werner Cole, please. Thank you."

There was a brief pause before Lt. Cole came to the phone. "Lt. Cole speaking."

"Hi, Lieutenant, it's Judge Collins."

"Yes, the man with the peaceful voice, the miracle worker. How are you doing, sir?" he replied in a surprised manner.

"Fine Werner, how's your wife Felicia and your daughter, Miriam? She must be about eight years old now."

"Exactly eight, your honor," he smiled. "Felicia will be so pleased you phoned. She still prays for you and the super-fast manner in which you expedited the adoption papers for our Miriam," he gushed. "What can I do for you, Judge?"

"First, convey my fondest regards to your wife and give an extra big hug to your daughter for me. And, I need a favor."

"Anything, anything," he promised.

"I need the name, address, and phone number of the person or persons with the following PA DMV registration."

"If it is active, I'll get it for you," he replied.

"Ready? OK...here it is: I JHN 5-2. Did you get it? That's right."

Cole asked sheepishly, "Will you be sending me an official request, Judge?"

178

"No actually, I can't send you anything on this officially. Let's just say I issued the court order and the record's been permanently sealed. Is that clear? Right. Would you handle this request personally, do the actual legwork yourself and call me with the information. No paperwork trail on either end. How long before you call back? Fifteen, twenty minutes would be just fine. Thanks, Lieutenant."

CHAPTER 12

Joan Evans sat at the edge of the bed. Her husband
Alan was completing his examination of the stitches that
stretched down the middle of her chest. He gingerly touched
them and declared, "God bless the medical profession and God
bless Dr. Laura Rankin." Joan smiled as she noticed that his
eyes lingered a long time to the right and left of her midline
chest incision. "Stitches look great, Joan," he added. "I didn't
realize Laura was both a great surgeon and supreme sewer of
bodies, no doubt a finalist in the Coates and Clark School of
Medicine. Makes me wonder how great a tattoo artist she
could have been if she failed med school." He was excited
about her progress and was looking forward to her returning to
their home. He looked into her eyes and added, "Can't wait 'til
you get home so I can count those stitches all day." Joan knew
what he was hinting at and told him "soon enough." Earlier he
had given her a folio of "Get well" wishes and love notes from
the children. Her room was adorned with a myriad of "Get
Well" notes and messages as well as a funeral parlor-type
assemblage of flowers and planters. "Make sure you read it to
mommy, in case her eyes are sore from the pills the hospital is
giving her," Amy reminded him as he left for the hospital. He
knelt at her feet as he adjusted the rubber knobby non-slip
hospital issued footwear. "There you are, ready to climb any
smooth surface!" He paused. "It's been over a week since you
said you wanted to visit Janice. Is today the day?"

"Yes, today is the day. But, I admit. I'm nervous."

"We're facing this together. Let's get going," he
encouraged.

She grabbed onto his arm and carefully slid from the
bed. Smilingly, they slowly walked out of the room and
proceeded down the hall past the tastefully decorated walls of
excellent copies of Whistler, Monet, and Sargent. She paused

at the van Gogh painting of the "Wheatfield with Crows" and correctly remarked, "What an odd painting for an ICU, I mean is it even appropriate for any hospital floor?" Janice Franco was on the same floor and had recovered to the point where she was taking regular walks around the hospital. Her planned release date coincided with Joan's.

Joan shuffled towards Janice's room. She hesitated as she knocked on the door jam and peered into the room. "Hello, Janice…"

"Hi, who's there," came a cheerful voice.

Joan and Alan entered the room to meet Janice. "Hi, Janice, I'm Joan Evans. We met when your child was born…I delivered your baby…"

****

It was an unusually warm and sunny April morning as Hewitt drove south on I-81. He smiled as he adjusted his sunglasses as he passed the fifth sign that warned drivers about the possibly notorious Fog Conditions on the highway. No problem with the fog this time he thought. He glanced at his watch and estimated he had another hour and a half before he arrived in Lancaster. He thought about the case. Hewitt was sure that the answer to the disappearances lay in the information he received from the State Police Motor Vehicle Identification system; if it wasn't the owners of the I JHN 5-2 license plate, then it was one of the other registrations beginning with "I J". He felt in control of the investigation.

Hewitt reasoned that the car that Grayson saw at the hospital that night must have been there to pick up Baby Franco from Dr. Nichols. The car was leaving as Grayson was arriving. Dr. Nichols was there, waiting for Grayson.

He glanced at the folder on the front seat of the car. "Stoltzfus, eh?" he said aloud. "Is that a Polish name, maybe German? Probably Catholic to boot, one of those pro-lifers, knows what's good for everyone else. Virtue in action."

181

Hewitt belonged to the largest segment of the Catholic faith, the lapsed Catholic or "Catholic, but I don't agree with the church's position on..." variety. When religion came up in conversation and he was asked to identify his faith, he would begin his answer in one of three ways: "I was born a Catholic, but..." or "My parents were Catholic, but..." or "I was baptized a Catholic, but..." He would never admit to being Catholic without pleading extenuating circumstances. When boiled down to their essence, those extenuating circumstances were simply an overriding disinterest in a spiritual life. Internally, he justified his position as stemming from an unavoidable disagreement with the Pope's position on virtually everything from the refugee crisis, to birth control, to just plain not liking his old style wardrobe.

It was nearly noon when he exited I-81 onto a local road that ran south towards Lancaster. He passed a sign that encouraged him to "Be a Star" and join the "table action" at nearby Hollywood Casino. "Not today," he thought to himself, turning south onto state route 72. He finally reached the city of Lancaster and navigated the streets crowded with tourists visiting art galleries and shopping at trendy boutiques. He made a mental note to revisit the town someday. He continued south on route 222. Several miles later, he moved to the shoulder and stopped to consult the directions he had been given by the state police. Satisfied that he had a mental picture of where to go, he continued. Shortly thereafter he took a left turn onto a secondary road. He followed the road for several miles.

He slowed down as he approached a farm on the left. From the road he could see a large almost oversized weather beaten wood frame farmhouse, an attached garage and a large barn with patchy newly mounted unpainted and roughhewn siding. Structurally, the house and garage looked sound but appeared to be in need of some dressing-up. Odd, nearly every other farmhouse along the way was in near perfect condition. Somehow, something was amiss. "Too much looks too

182

staged," he thought to himself.

"Shabby on the outside, a ruse" he asked himself, or "maybe shabby chic," he added? He pulled the car to the side of the road as he surveyed the rest of the property. He reached for his binoculars.

"Barn's in good shape for a barn. H'm'm two newly hung sliding doors that look rather large." He thought to himself that an average barn door is about 12 feet high but these look larger, say 16 feet. "And, what, recently installed Anderson replacement windows on the farmhouse's second level? Haven't removed the factory stickers. Not adding up. H'm'm, no livestock in sight, no chickens, not even a dog or the typical roaming cat, and where are the kids," he murmured aloud. "Well, drove all this way. Might as well stop in for a visit."

No one came out to greet him when he ascended the porch stairs. No one answered his knock at the door.

"A three-goddamn-hour drive and no one is home," he muttered, stepping back off the porch and looking to the second floor of the farmhouse.

"Anybody home?" he called out. "Hello, anybody here?" No response. He again went to the porch and knocked, harder this time, on the front door. "Hello. Anybody home?" He continued to knock and call out until he was convinced that no one was home.

"Anybody mind if I have a little look around the place?" he said aloud. "No response. Well then, let's see what we can see." He walked to each of the windows fronting the porch. The shades were drawn on each. He could not see inside. He stepped off the porch and examined the second-floor windows. Those shades were drawn as well. It was the same story on the left side of the house. At the rear of the house there was a solid wooden fence at least eight feet high surrounding the large area that abutted the garage. He observed it wasn't just a wooden fence but one finished in a craftsman-like manner. "Very high end," he surmised.

"What the hell!" he said. He stepped away from the fence and surveyed the surrounding area for a high enough vantage point to see over the fence. A nearby maple tree offered a promising perch. He jumped for an overhead branch and clumsily swung his legs onto a parallel branch. "I'm too old for this stuff," he said aloud hoping no one would hear him. He groped for a sturdy higher branch that was in front of him and slowly pulled himself to a seated position. He caught his pants on a sprig and tore a small hole in the seat. "Damn," he shouted. Had anyone been watching, they would have recognized that it had been a while since Hewitt had done any serious tree climbing. He fidgeted on his perch about eleven feet off the ground until he was facing the fence, now some 30 feet away.

He could see a gently sloping ramp leading from the back door to the yard. In the yard he saw some odd-looking playground equipment. Low-to-the-ground swings with high-back chairs suspended from chains…a gazebo with ramp, a large two-level western frontier-type fort with wide doors on each level and a platform elevator with a control post on the platform and on the ground. The platform was framed by what appeared to be a heavy-duty nylon mesh cage that had folding doors to allow a wheelchair to enter or exit from either side. The platform was large enough to enable a wheelchair to get to the second tier of the fort. He then realized that all the playground equipment was handicapped accessible and judging from the size of all the equipment, was small enough for child's play.

Hewitt left the tree as gracefully as he could, hanging by his arms before dropping to the ground and stumbling a bit. He continued to snoop around the house. Every window shade on the house was drawn, but not on the garage windows. The garage door was locked, so Hewitt went to the side of the building, stood on tiptoe, and, with his hands touching the glass and framing his face, he looked through the small unobstructed garage window.

The inside of the garage was immaculate. There was not a spot of oil or grease on the cement floor. Hewitt judged the garage hadn't housed a car since the floor was put in. The interior garage walls had been finished and painted light taupe. Drawings of various barnyard animals were stenciled on the wall opposite his view. There was a dropped ceiling in the garage. Flush with the ceiling surface were lighting fixture panels. There were several upright freezers along the far wall. A stainless steel counter top and sink formed a work area that would look right at home in a college chemistry lab. To the left of the sink he could see what he thought was a bookcase. Then he realized they were multi-colored metal shelves. Each of the four shelves had boxes on them. Each shelf had a different size box, but all the boxes on a particular shelf were exactly the same. Hewitt struggled, but failed to read the print on the boxes.

He then stood flat-footed at the side of the garage once more. He worked his way to the back of the garage. He looked at the industrial air conditioning unit for a full minute, assuming the unit was for the house and wondering why it was put in such an inconvenient location. But it was in the most convenient location for its purpose. The garage was air-conditioned. And even though it was April, and barely 72 degrees out, the air-conditioning unit was running.

He walked around the property and continued to the barn's lower level and looked into the unfinished dirt basement. "A work in progress," he thought. The frame and basic roughhewn siding were completed. Like many barns in the area the large barn doors were on the same level with the surrounding landscape but the basement for the dirt floor was accessible from a lower level of the land. He walked upwards to the main level and glanced into the partially open barn door. It was dark. He squeezed through without opening the door any further and took a step and peered around. "Can't see for the dark," he said annoyingly. He felt hopelessly for a light switch on the wall near the door but instead bruised his hand on a nail. "Damn unfinished interior side," he correctly surmised. He took another step and placed his foot in midair and tumbled through the hay hole opening of the rough framing of the unfinished floor to the crawl level space part of the ground floor. He tumbled down the dirt ramp. "Shit, shit, double shit," he yelled as he painfully slowly rose from the dirt floor brushing the dirt from his clothes. He heard the flitter of disturbed bats above him. He felt lucky that he had fallen through the section where he did because the dirt floor was only three feet from the barn floor level but angled down another 10 feet to the base construction level.

He looked around. There were several large 55-gallon steel drums placed along the side wall of the dirt level. He glanced at an electrical panel on the wall and, although only a weekend electrician thought that the wattage seemed overly sufficient for a barn, actually more suited for a large apartment house. Scattered around was a myriad of stainless steel pipes, ropes, electrical pumps, and the like. "Looks like a drilling rig down here," he thought.

He continued his mental inventory but, battered and bruised, he decided it was time to leave the farm. On his way back to the car Hewitt noticed the newly painted dumpster. "What the hell," he said. "After the tree, this will be a snap."

It wasn't. The dumpster lid was locked. "What the hell is this," said Hewitt aloud swatting the lock. "Either they've got some huge raccoons around here, or they don't want anyone to see what's in here. What's going on?"

He decided to pry the lid up so he could see inside the dumpster. Returning to his car for the tire iron he noticed a battered rust red Chevy pickup truck slow down as it approached the driveway to the farm and then speed up. "Can't be the residents," he muttered. "They would have pulled in to see who was here. Might be a neighbor though, they might call the police. That's no problem for me, as long as they don't shoot first and ask questions later." He looked at his watch. "Damn, it's after three already. I've got to get moving."

Tire iron in hand, he trotted back to the dumpster. He decided he would explain his assignment to the local police if they showed up, but he wouldn't tell them about his tour around the property or his efforts to open the dumpster. All in all, he intended to be gone before the locals showed up. Back at the dumpster he attempted to pry the lid open slightly. The tire iron lost the lip of the dumpster and slipped out of Hewitt's hand, dropping to the ground. Hewitt knelt to retrieve the tire iron. That's when he saw the piece of cardboard. He picked it up. The cardboard had a ripped, transparent plastic sleeve on it and contained a folded pink sheet of paper. Hewitt pulled the paper from the sleeve.

"Universal Pharmaceutical," read Hewitt. "This is not an invoice. It's a packing slip..." Hewitt paused while he searched for the order number. "Fine, no order number." He looked at the long list of items ordered from Universal Pharmaceutical. "Man," said Hewitt. "There are enough drugs here to run a hospital."

He looked up at the farmhouse, and down at the slip, and up at the farmhouse, then the garage. "Enough drugs to run a hospital, for sure." He turned toward his car and broke into a run, clutching the tire iron, cardboard, and packing slip. He quickly slid into the driver's seat.

Hewitt decided he would wait until he was back on the main road before calling the Chief and Silva and have them schedule a search warrant hearing with Judge Collins. They also needed to work out a cooperate arrangement with the local Lancaster sheriff. The warrant would allow him a long hard look at the Stoltzfus' house, garage, barn and dumpster. Hewitt was mentally preparing his arguments for Chief Wallington and Silva and did not notice the battered rust red Chevy pickup truck increasing in size in his rearview mirror.

****

Nearly 12 hours later the phone next to Chief

Wallington's bed rang, waking the chief from a sound sleep. He was accustomed to receiving early morning phone calls. It was part of his job. He prided himself on his ability to be alert and clear-headed immediately upon being awakened. Dispatchers who contacted him in the middle of the night were often left with the distinct impression that the chief had been sitting by the phone waiting for them to call.

"Wallington here. What have you got for me?"

"Chief Wallington?" said the voice on the other end of the phone.

"Himself," said Wallington, recalling the matter of self-addressing speech oft used by a local Irish tavern owner. "Now, what can I do for you?"

"Chief, this is Sergeant Alex Tucker, Lancaster, PA. Police Department."

"Yes," he answered wondering if he was on a solicitation list for police Kevlar vest funding.

"Well, it seems like one of your boys had an accident down our way, banged himself up pretty bad."

"Hewitt."

"That's him. Hewitt. Well, sir, like I said, he's banged up. They got him over to Lancaster General Hospital."

"What happened? How bad is it?"

"Don't know exactly what happened. No witnesses. But a passing motorist found your boy in a ditch off to the side of one of our back roads a few hours ago. Appears he had wrapped his car around a pine tree pretty good. But they tell me the doctors say he'll be OK, and you should worry none. They've been working on him for a whiles now."

Wallington smiled at the dialect. "I appreciate the call, Sergeant. Would you please repeat what you said and give me the particulars about the hospital again? And listen, would you mind posting a guard outside Hewitt's room, and secure the accident scene?"

"Was your boy up to something out here? We have no information on a cooperative venture."

"No, Sarge," lied the chief. "He's been working on a rough case up here involving some boys who may have connections. You know what I mean. Big city types with last names that end in vowels. Anyway, he was beginning to draw some unwelcome attention. I wanted him to get out of town for a few days. And since he is a sucker for a hefty smorgasbord, he decided to do some sightseeing down your way. Someone may have followed him."

"So what are we looking for?"

"Probably nothing. But until I talk to Hewitt, I'd rather be safe than sorry. Just post someone outside his door and get a positive ID from anyone who goes into his room, including all medical personnel. Maintain a log of all persons entering that room, time in, time out, and purpose of visit. You know what I mean. That should be enough to discourage anyone out to mess with him."

"OK, Chief, can do."

After finishing with the Lancaster call, Wallington called Prosecutor Silva.

"Hello," answered Silva sleepily.

"Henry, this is the chief. Hewitt's been in an accident. He's in Lancaster General Hospital."

"Lord, what happened?"

"He was checking out that lead, the license plate thing."

"Did Hewitt coordinate his little excursion with the local authorities?"

"No, Henry. My fault, I'm afraid. I told him I'd contact Lancaster PD and I forgot. Spending too much time counting the days to retirement."

"Right. That's your story and you're sticking to it, am I correct?"

"That's right, Mr. Prosecutor."

"So we had an officer poking around in another jurisdiction without anyone there knowing about it, and that officer ends up in the hospital."

"That's about the size of it, Henry. That's the least of my concerns. I want to bring Dr. Nichols in."

"What, tonight?"

"Now."

"Hold on, hold on. Let's see. Give me a few minutes. I have to talk to Judge Collins."

"What the hell for?"

"Ah, he made me promise that we'd contact that Bedford woman before we made any public announcements or any arrests in the case."

"That's bullshit, Henry. Complete bullshit. I don't need the judge's permission to arrest this guy, and I certainly don't have to check in with some civilian woman..."

"Look, the judge was really pissed last time around when we didn't notify the mother about the exhumation results. He can be a real bulldog, and you don't want to get that bulldog mad at you."

"Call him then," snapped the chief, "but I'm dispatching a car to Nichols's place right now. We won't touch him till the judge OKs it, but Nichols will have company wherever he goes from here on out."

****

"Absolutely not," said Judge Collins. "As soon as you arrest Nichols the press will be all over this, reporters will be contacting the families. Let the poor woman have a good night's sleep so she can deal with all this. Hold off a couple of hours."

"But Judge, what if Hewitt's accident wasn't an accident?"

"You've got no indication it was anything other than an accident. Anyway, Nichols is the guy you want. You know where he is. You've got a squad car outside his house. He's not going anywhere. You can afford to wait a couple of hours. I'll call Grace Bedford at 7 a.m. Have Chief

190

Wallington arrest Nichols at 7:15 and not a minute sooner, understand?"

"What do I get out of this deal?"

"Henry, when you want to call in this chip, we'll talk. But there's just no reason to disturb that poor woman in the dead of night."

"OK, Judge. But if I get shot tonight, make sure someone takes a real close look at the chief's alibi."

"Agreed."

****

At 7:15 a.m. Chief Joseph Wallington rang the doorbell at the home of Dr. Frederick Nichols. Nichols came to the door fully dressed.

"Dr. Nichols," said the chief.

"Yes, detective, what is it?"

"I am placing you under arrest for the kidnapping of the Franco infant. You have the right to remain silent..."

****

Joan Evans pushed her breakfast tray aside while Janice Franco was mopping up the last of her two over light eggs with a piece of toast splattered with orange marmalade. Joan felt a kinship to Janice, sort of a big sister, someone to watch over. The bonding was more meaningful and heartfelt than a doctor-patient relationship. This was their third hospital meal together. They had shared much. There was so much more to Janice than simply the accident victim who delivered a handicapped baby. That in itself was courageous and noteworthy.

They talked about her dreams; she felt she had a calling in life. She believed that although she appeared ramshackle, unaccountable, and reckless; she told Joan that she wanted to continue her education. She wanted to save

191

enough money to enter a profession. She had always wanted to become a Licensed Practical Nurse. She envisioned herself working at rural medical clinic or senior living facility. She wanted to help people. In fact, she had an upcoming interview at a county-sponsored nursing program in Scranton; but besides a money shortfall, her primary concern about the interview was her right arm. She admitted that it was the result of one helluva crazy night somewhere in New Mexico! A meticulously completed sleeve tattoo, it pictured a myriad of multi-colored snakes and thick jungle vines down the length of her arm. "That artistry was the result of too much tequila, a fabulously looking Hispanic guy, too much sex, and a dare!" she smiled. "But now, that damn tattoo could be my downfall!"

She also told Joan that she read a lot of books…in fact, she was on book "S" of the encyclopedia. "Yes, I started reading from book "A" and found it exciting. For example did you know that Mt. Everest was 29,028 feet high and growing?" And she smiled when she crowed she had "aced" the admission practice tests for the nursing program. Joan promised to make a phone call on her behalf.

Joan enjoyed her company. "A real, authentic, fun-loving but serious young lady," she characterized. "If anyone judged her by her looks, they would miss the gem that lies within," she added. Compared to Janice's life, Joan's was a dream. She could list prep school, college, and med schools to her credit. But her education was more planned and regimented, more precise and scheduled, than the thirst for knowledge Janice must have had to undertake the reading of the encyclopedia. Joan judged Janice's determination to succeed and learn was eons beyond her persona. She admired Janice. And so she chose not to elaborate on her academic accomplishments because it would seem more bragging than sharing. She didn't want to compete with Janice, she wanted to bond with her.

Thoughtfully, Joan approached the gorilla in the

room, the one she knew all too well. She decided that she wanted Janice to know something the dwelt deep within her. She decided to share her pain, the loss she still felt as the result of the abortion and the forever lost hours of nursing her baby. She talked about the mistakes she had made when she was younger and the nightmares that plagued her. She described that the pain of the forfeiture of her involvement in her child's life was unbearable at times. Her thoughts and sharing cornered the market on "what if" and "what could have been" when she saw mothers walking and talking with their 10-year old children. Even looking at the 10-year-olds modeling clothing in fashion magazines tore at her.

Janice reached for her hand. "You know Dr. Evans..."

"Please call me Joan," she interrupted.

"That might be difficult but I'll try. You know...Joan... maybe I'm too young to fully absorb the full impact of the loss of my child. I grieve, yes, but I believe in the God-given strength he sends us in time of need. I remember reading in the Britannica under the letter "P", she smiled, "that in physics equilibrium exists when one force pushes against an equal force with the same intensity that that force exerts on it. Not a precise explanation, but I think you get the idea..."

"I'm not following you,"

"God gives us the strength not to succumb to our brokenness, or loss, our problems. He gives us the strength to equalize and grow from life's tragedies with his grace, enabling us to carry on, to rise above...with his added strength...I call it a 'double grace whammy'- A combination of actual grace for those one time inspirations or motivations that move us along, and sanctifying grace for sustainability in living in the world, sort of to keep us paddling our canoe down the river of life." She smiled at her description then added, "Yikes, I sound like a college professor!""

Another light went on in Joan's soul. "Janice, I think I get it!" She thought of the confession with Fr. Charles and smiled. "Thank you, dear one…"

"So, our loss is complemented, with an 'e' instead of an 'i', by an almighty, all-knowing, all merciful Holy One."

Joan's eyes started to tear. "I think I understand. I understand." She smiled a thankful, forgiven smile. The moment wasn't lost on either of them.

"We're loved so we can accept or tolerate or move on with life in spite of our loss," Joan added.

"Well, maybe it isn't that easy but we can move on because of our loss."

"Janice, you remind me of another physician in this hospital who believes the way you do. One who walks the walk. Who believes in the power of God. I must thank him for his determination, his sort of evangelical spirit, but not his annoying nature," she laughed. She decided she wanted to talk with Dr. Nichols again.

CHAPTER 13

The arrest of Doctor Nichols on kidnapping charges generated immense interest in the press. Representative contingents from major newspapers, TV and radio networks, and wire services descended upon Honesdale. National Public Radio broke the story that three other similar cases, all involving Dr. Nichols, were being investigated.

Henry Silva, while not yet comfortable in the role, was becoming adept at handling reporters' questions during press conferences. Personally, he enjoyed acknowledging a reporter simply by the nod of his head. He wondered if this was how Roman Emperors ruled, a turn of the wrist, a nod of the head, a smirk here, a thumbs down there. Unconsciously, he looked around for a throne.

The desire to uncover the big story, an exclusive, lives in the heart of every journalist. However, the greater motivating factor in the gathering of all news is the fear of being beaten, even on a minor detail, by the competition. The "thrill of the kill" was alive in every profession. By conducting two briefings each day, Silva was able to keep the reporters tethered to the courthouse and in fairly tight quarters. In this way the ladies and gentlemen of the press could do their jobs with minimal effort and keep their eyes on each other.

This tact was aided by the reluctance of the defense to come out and play. Dr. Nichols was arraigned and out on bail within two hours of his arrest. He and his attorney, Jim Fallon, had to run a minor gauntlet of cameras, microphones, and a jumble of shouted questions following the arraignment. All the reporters agreed that Dr. Nichols was possibly the worst interviewee in the history of journalism, but they shouted their questions at him anyway, hoping against hope that Jim Fallon would respond and give them some footage or a decent sound bite or quote.

"Doctor, what did you do with the bodies?" shouted one reporter.

"Doctor, some are comparing you with Dr. Mengele, the Nazi physician who conducted medical experiments on Jews and other prisoners of the Third Reich. Any comment?" called the young handsome TV reporter who had been working on correctly pronouncing Dr. Mengele's name; a name he had learned earlier that day.

"My client is innocent of all charges," said Fallon, standing by his car after Dr. Nichols had entered the relative seclusion of the passenger's seat. "Completely innocent. We'll have a more detailed statement later. Now, if you please, we need to be on our way."

"Did you hear those questions?" asked Dr. Nichols.

"Don't let them get to you, Doctor. They're calculated to create a reaction. They don't much care what kind of reaction, just as long as you react. It beefs up the video if you turn angrily and scream at them. The whole world wants a sound bite. The question that caused the reaction will never be mentioned, only your reaction will make it to YouTube. You did well, very well."

"What do we do now?"

"Well, we draft a statement," said Fallon. Dr. Nichols gave him an angry look. "Don't worry about it; I'll take care of it. Just a brief statement reiterating your innocence and saying how confident you are that the investigation will ultimately clear you of all charges. I'll show it to you when we get to the house. I have a draft of the statement in my briefcase."

"You have a statement written already?"

"Don't take this the wrong way Doctor, but this part of the case is routine. We try to make what case we can with the press without over-exposing ourselves. Remember that our best scenario is that this whole thing goes away. That's not going to happen. So we give the press something, but not much. You'll be staying behind closed doors, if you care to follow my advice..."

"That seems quite appealing to me right now."

"Good. Now understand this. When we get to the house, there will likely be another contingent of reporters waiting for us. I don't want you to say anything. We walk to the front door, we go in. I come out a few minutes later and give them a little talk. But don't expect them to go away."

"What are you saying? I'm going to have reporters in my front yard from now on?"

"For a while anyway you can expect at least one or two to be there around the clock."

"Well, they'd better stay off my property."

"I'll make that clear to them," said Fallon. "Now obviously, if they're out there all the time they'll swoop down on you every time you go in or out. So, my advice is: stay in. Let them swoop down on me as I come and go. They get their few seconds of videotape and you stay out of sight."

****

"I can't believe I'm stuck in this hospital talking to you via facetime and all hell is breaking loose," said Daniel Hewitt from his Lancaster hospital bed.

"Now, Dan," said Chief Wallington, "take it easy. You've had a rough day. Besides, you're not missing a thing. We arrested Nichols and we've got Grayson in protective custody. That was his request after we told him about your accident."

"That was no accident," said Hewitt. "That pickup deliberately ran me off the road."

"I believe you, son, I believe you. But without a plate number, looking for a beat-up Chevy pickup down there is like looking for a cornfield in Kansas. Anyway, Nichols was out on bail before I got here. Damndest thing. He's got this attorney from Connecticut who just happened to be in town."

"Really."

"Yeah. Got in town yesterday, according to the hotel records," said the chief.

"We've got a mole, Chief."

"How do you figure?"

"Someone tipped off the house I went to yesterday. Everyone was gone. Place was empty, not even a barking dog. I bet the barn mice had left the area, too. I was set up for this pickup to try and kill me. And to top it off, Dr. Nichols's out-of-state attorney just happens to be in town when you arrest him."

"You know, Dan, there is such a thing as being too suspicious, even for a cop. Nichols's attorney arrived yesterday. He was in town before you got down here. He's some hotshot lawyer. He and Nichols run in the same circles.

"OK, what about the truck?"

"You said yourself a beat-up red pickup came by the house while you were there. So the bad guys were out when you got to the house. They came back, saw you there, waited till you left and then ran you off the road. No mole necessary."

"I guess you're right."

"I know I am, Dan. The important thing is that you take it easy for a few days."

"I can't stay in here for a few days. Look, I'm fine, a little groggy. But no worse than when I pull one of those all-nighters and am back at work the next morning."

"Dan, you had a compound fracture of your left leg. You lost a lot of blood. They figure you were in that wreck for seven hours before someone came by. Man, that's one lonely stretch of road."

"The leg's in a cast. They are giving me some very good drugs here. I've arrested guys for holding stuff that wasn't nearly this good. I can use a wheelchair to get around the farmhouse. As for the blood, if I was a quart low, they put a quart back in. Good blood, I trust. No Hep-C or whatever. So, blood problem solved. We've got to get back to that house with

198

a search warrant. I'm telling you they're running a hospital there. This Dr. Nichols and whomever he's working with are there. They tried to kill me, and they probably will try to kill me again."

"And you base this on what?" asked Wallington.

"Bad things seem to happen to people who question what Dr. Nichols is up to. Evans was on to him, she knew Baby Franco wasn't dying, she accused Nichols of falsifying the medical charts, and I'm sure she'll put that in writing when she feels better."

"She had a heart attack, no one tried to kill her. But since you are lost in a world of paranoia, who, exactly, are the *they* you are accusing of attempted murder?"

"Nichols, the driver in the red pickup truck, the Stoltzfus', whoever's in that house. This is no rinky-dink operation. You had to see that lab, the refrigeration units, all the high-end assorted medical and playground equipment. The stainless steel apparatus that was stacked in the barn must have cost a pretty penny, too. They're organized and have the money to finance this thing of theirs."

"Look," said the chief, "you've got to calm down. I've spoken with the doctors down there. They won't consider letting you out of the hospital before tomorrow and they aren't crazy about doing it even then, but if you lie down and make like a good little patient we can probably spring you tomorrow." Wallington focused more seriously, "Look, I believe in some of the things you say, not all, but where there's smoke, there's fire. I'm planning to drive to Lancaster, I'll take a couple of guys out to the farm myself as soon as I get there. We'll have to go out there without you."

"You won't see much without a search warrant, and we can't get a warrant until I can get out of this place and return to Honesdale."

"That's no problem," said Henry Silva, who had just entered the Chief's office. "We'll conduct a bedside hearing, then a warrant is issued and the Chief and I go look this place over with a few local gendarmes. How are you doing, Dan?"

"Hello, Mr. Prosecutor. How the hell are you?"

"Better than you, Dan. You look uglier than usual."

"So do you," said Dan, "but someone tried to kill me with a truck. What's your excuse?"

"Worrying about you, my boy," said Silva. "How's our guy doing, Chief?"

"All in all, not much different. Same charming disposition anyway. Nice to see you, Henry. What's the deal with a bedside hearing?"

"In a sentence we bring a local judge to Dan's room, Dan gives a sworn statement in support of the search warrant. The judge issues the search warrant, and we go out to the house with local authorities."

"How soon can we do it?" asked Hewitt.

"I've made the call to the local prosecutor. One judge talks with another, the wheels move in a circular motion…"

"Something like Mr. Toad's Wild Ride," Hewitt interjected sarcastically, "up and down, over an across, we hang on tight and we wind up at the same place where we began!"

"Judge should be there soon," said Silva.

"Just exactly how'd you manage that?" asked the Chief admiringly.

"Well, it took some arguing. Judge Collins owed me a favor. He balked at first. I tell you, this case has his panties all in a knot. Ever since he decided to call that Bedford woman about the exhumation, he's been more concerned with her mental health than anything else. He didn't like the idea, but he finally gave in and contacted the assignment judge down there. The short version is: a Judge Fisher and a court stenographer will be here soon to take your testimony in support of a search warrant for this farmhouse slash hospital you say you found."

Within an hour Judge Fisher issued the search warrant based on Grayson's sworn statement, which Silva had e-mailed to Fisher and on Hewitt's sworn testimony concerning his investigation of Dr. Nichols and what he had seen at the farmhouse.

****

Jim Fallon parked his car in Dr. Nichols's driveway. The cluster of reporters surged toward him as he got out of his car.

"The prosecutor's office says it has not ruled out the possibility that Detective Hewitt's accident may be related to this case. Do you have any comment?" This question could be heard above the others shouted at Fallon, in part because the reporter was the closest to Fallon, but mostly because it was the only question Fallon was interested in responding to.

"I have no reason, and I do not believe the prosecutor's office has any reason, to believe that there is any connection between Detective Hewitt's unfortunate accident and the false charges that have been brought against my client. As far as we know, Detective Hewitt could have suffered the consequences of a two martini lunch. I'm not saying he did, but the facts are twisted and unclear at this time. An accident is an accident."

"So you say Detective Hewitt's accident was just an accident?"

"I am saying I have absolutely no reason to believe otherwise."

"What about the prosecutor's statement?"

"He did not say there was a connection. He only said he had not yet ruled it out. We regret that the prosecutor has not yet had the time to adequately look into the matter but we are confident that once he does, he will, in fact, rule out any connection."

"How is Dr. Nichols?"

"Well, that is what I'm about to find out. We've spoken by phone several times today and I'd have to say he's doing well, considering the very trying circumstances. Now if you'll excuse me."

"Mr. Fallon, one more question, please."

"I'm sorry, catch me on the way out. I'm here to confer with my client," said Fallon, smiling and waving to the reporters who continued to shout questions to him as he knocked on the door of Dr. Nichols's home.

"This is the oddest experience," said Dr. Nichols as Fallon slipped through the partially opened door.

"What would that be?" asked Fallon as Dr. Nichols closed the door.

"I'm sitting in my living room watching a local TV station and they suddenly cut away from the show for a live feed and then I find myself sitting in my house watching my lawyer speaking to reporters in front of my house. It has a very surreal quality to it."

"How'd I do?"

"I don't know how you do it."

"I've told you before. Stay in control, don't react, unless the reaction works in your favor. It isn't that hard for me to do. After all, every time I come here, or go to the courthouse or go to my hotel room I expect to be accosted by reporters. So, expecting to be ambushed I am prepared, I have this invincible body armor. They can flail about and hurl anything they like at me. I'm ready for them. As the poet wrote: affliction is the good man's shining time."

"Of course the ability to keep your cool may have something to do with the fact that you're not the one facing jail time if you lose the case," said Dr. Nichols.

"That does permit me to maintain a certain distance from these events that my clients cannot," said Fallon. "That is why I have asked that you remain here and let me come to you."

"Fedderson only suggested that I be boring and cough a lot."

"It's an effective short term approach if your goal is to be ignored by the press. However, as often as not, my role is to get a point across to the press. I must be concise, accessible, and charming unless the circumstances call for apt righteous indignation."

"Being holed up here gives me a lot of time to think. If I'm convicted I'll never practice medicine again. And my work with the network, that must end as well. But my problems are not the important issue here. If we don't get this fiasco under control, it could put an end to the entire resurrection network."

"True. You have some difficult choices ahead of you," said Fallon. "The reason I came by was to tell you about a call I received from the *New York Times*," said Fallon.

"Yes?" said Dr. Nichols.

"They wanted a comment about a story they intend to run in tomorrow's edition."

"What's the story?"

"They claim to have sources alleging you are part of a wide ranging and well-funded conspiracy involving doctors and others who "rescue" infant patients for whom life sustaining treatment is to be removed."

"They know about the network! What are we going to do? What did you tell them?"

"I told them the idea was preposterous and a symptom of the type of paranoia that is rampant in our society today. Everything is a conspiracy."

"But what happens once the *Times* prints the story? Won't it draw a lot of attention?"

"By tomorrow morning you can expect all hell to break loose. This is a big story with one missing infant. The press now knows about three other possible incidents, all handled by the same doctor and funeral home and it smacks of some grand conspiracy, which of course, to be sure, it is. Now the *Times* say some sort of secret underground organization is involved. You can expect to draw representatives from every major media outlet in the U.S. There would be worldwide attention for a while. And you can also count on the usual cast of characters who have an ax to grind to set up shop in this very public forum. There will be supporters and detractors picketing in front of your house, in front of the hospital, in front of the funeral home, in front of any news camera they can manage to get in front of. Pro-life, pro-choice, and a generous sampling of kooks and weirdoes grasping for their 15 minutes of fame. We'll attract friends and enemies. We'll be a magnet for the sincere, the misguided, and the deluded.

Nichols added, "It will be a time of polarization run amuck, sort of to say."

"We might be able to lessen some of the street circus aspects if we work the trial schedule into the winter months. We'd need a very cold winter, but not much snow. Cold enough to keep the kooks inside, but not so inclement that we lose trial days."

"It hardly seems as if hoping for bad weather is a sterling legal defense."

"It all comes into play. Let's not forget, Doctor, you are guilty. That does tend to complicate things. And consider this: it may be that having this story break now works in your favor. It was bound to come out at trial anyway. If it comes out now, it could be old news by trial time. Sometimes these things flare up and burn themselves out within a few weeks. It all depends on what else is happening out there, a terrorist attack here, a presidential scandal there, the collapse of the European community. Any number of things could knock us off the front pages."

"And O.J. could find the real murderer," said Dr. Nichols.

Fallon didn't respond.

"So this could burn itself out in a few weeks, or," said Nichols.

"Or it could go on for months, or for years. I was hoping to avoid this information getting out. This is the type of exposure that puts the Network at risk. I think you know that under these circumstances, it will be very difficult for the Network to continue operating. And this is just the beginning of the exposure. Once the press gets on the trail of something like this they can make things very unpleasant. Very difficult. We need an escape hatch. Some way to end it all. A final solution, if you will."

"Final solution?" asked Dr. Nichols.

"Yes, it would be best if there was some way to end it right here. Right now. Avoid the pre-trial motions, the press coverage, the additional investigations, and the trial."

"I've assured you I won't talk. There is nothing they can do to make me talk."

"We know you won't, Doctor. You're the kind of man who knows his duty. We know that you would do anything to preserve the Network."

"What about the Stoltzfus'?"

"A very near mishap. If we hadn't received that phone call before Hewitt arrived he would have seen the children. They barely had time to secure the place and get out. We've taken steps to cover their trail completely. No more vanity license plates, I can tell you that, Dr. Nichols. For a while the network will have to keep its light under the bushel basket. With luck, we'll be able to emerge again and get back to work."

"What about Hewitt's accident?" asks Nichols.

"What about it?"

"How accidental was it?"

"All I can tell you is that," said Fallon, "some were disappointed in the attempt, others with the result."

"So we're willing to risk lives, are we? That's what we've come to."

"Dr. Nichols, we are at war. In war there are casualties. I'm never surprised, nor saddened really, when some errant fanatic decides to remove one of these abortionists…"

"I don't like the sound of that. That's not who I am or what I'm about. The Network is about saving lives, not encouraging collateral damage."

"Think of all the lives they have taken. The innocent blood spilled. When you consider the holocaust they caused.

Legally the Constitution is in shambles, and morally the country is a vacuous space yearning to be filled with truth and substance. The only surprising thing is really that more of them are not brought to justice. We can't control everyone who believes in pro-life issues. There are people on the periphery looking for ways to help us, wanting to be a part of something. Sometimes they initiate what we would consider reckless acts. We don't condone those acts, but understand the frustration and their guilt."

"Guilt? What do you mean by their guilt?"

"Everyone wants to be a hero. Everyone wants to have their day in the sun. We all want to be an honoree at a banquet, receive a medal, and stand to a round of applause."

"Not everyone, Jim. Not everyone. Belief in the Network is moral; action in the Network ought to be morality in action."

These nonprofessionals can't be depended on to remain silent if caught, so it's best if they don't know exactly who or what is directing them."

"It's true, then. We've become what we abhor."

"Doctor, please. Let's look at this pragmatically. More than 50-million babies murdered in America since *Rowe v. Wade*. Fifty million! How many abortionists have been killed? A handful. Would it be so terrible if every abortionist had died and those 50-million innocent lives had been spared?"

"I did not get involved in the Resurrection Network to kill or even delve in the mental 'what ifs' that that kind of thinking involves," said Dr. Nichols. "My sole purpose was to save lives."

"And you have, Doctor. Remember, one of your earliest cases still lives. His is a difficult life, but one filled with love and caring. And the lives he has changed! It's true what DeVinck wrote about the power of the powerless. You made those years of love possible. Without your intervention society would have murdered that child for convenience's sake. And there are scores of other similar successes throughout the Resurrection Network. We are active in every state. We save dozens of lives every year. That's what makes this so difficult. All of those successes, all our future work, at risk if this case goes on. Is it such a bad thing to purchase the lives of so many children with a few lives of those who would murder them? Is our own life so precious to us that we would prefer to live and let the network die? If the Network fails, it will be like giving the death sentence to hundreds of children."

"And those responsible for the Network's failure would be responsible for killing those children?"

"Exactly, Doctor. Innocent blood would be on their hands."

"What if the case did not go to trial, perhaps if I were to plead guilty?"

"You want to plead guilty?"

"If there were a guilty plea, and I maintain my silence, wouldn't all this end?"

"It isn't that simple, Dr. Nichols. For the plea to be accepted the judge will insist on a complete account of your role. That includes naming any accomplices. If the judge thinks you're holding back, he can order you to go to trial. And the prosecution would have the opportunity to present their version of the facts in open court. It would be worse than a trial, they'd get to present their case and we'd have very little room for rebuttal."

"A guilty plea wouldn't put an end to it."

"No, I am afraid not."

"So what do we do?"

"There are options. We could put up a hell of a fight. Challenge every aspect of their case. We might be able to raise the doctor-patient privilege issue in pre-trial motions. Maybe take that all the way to the Supreme Court. That could eat up a year or two. Most likely we'd lose, of course. In each of the cases the parents or guardians had the right to speak for the patient. In effect they are the patient so the privilege would not hold. We'd look a little foolish, but we could delay things for quite a while."

"And the press coverage..."

"That will continue, I'm afraid. Each new motion, each court appearance, each press conference by the prosecutor would present an opportunity to rehash the entire story. And the longer the case went on, the greater the chances are the network would be exposed."

"Everything we have accomplished is at risk because a drunken father insisted on seeing the body of a child he couldn't have cared less about," said Nichols reflectively as he shook his head. "I appreciate your taking the time to walk me through the legal aspects of this situation, Jim. Now it's time for morality in action."

"I hear you Fred."

"What do you suggest?"

"I spoke with Phil Duran earlier today. He mapped several scenarios after talking with the boss. Since that time and with the *Times* story breaking only one scenario is viable." He reached into his briefcase and withdrew a handgun – a Ruger SR22. He handed it to Nichols. "This is our best answer to a terrible problem."

"What am I supposed to do with this?" shouted Nichols.

"You leave a brief note…and pull the trigger. Problem solved. In fact, I've taken the liberty of writing the note for you. Saves you time to prepare to meet the big man."

Nichols sat in astonishment. He looked at the handgun. "I've never fired a gun before. Will this take care of everything?"

"It's not a heavyweight gun, Fred. It's a .22 caliber. It'll go bang and make a smallish hole where it hits. The bullet is smaller than say, a .38 caliber Colt. It'll do the job we want. But, Fred the note is revealing. Rather dicey, actually. Hopefully, it won't be an embarrassment to you or others. But we need to buy you a little more time. Some people will be looking for you; others will be examining the contents of the note, looking for further clues, more dirt, and the like. In any event our exit strategy is sound."

"This is OK with Duran?"

"The boss approved the plan, also."

"OK then. The letter…where do I sign and how do I use this gun?"

"Take a minute to review the note. Sign your name at the bottom."

"Thanks, Jim."

"See you on the other side, friend. But let's wait an hour or so, at least until the press outside decides to go home for the night. The fewer the better, you understand. Take no prisoners, no witnesses."

Fallon gave Nichols the letter and showed him how to hold the gun and where to place the barrel for maximum effect. The plan called for Nichols to go into the den with the letter, point and pull the trigger when ready. Fallon would call 911 and the hospital EMT squad would respond. Convinced that Nichols was able to execute the plan, he walked to the kitchen and made a cup of coffee.

Nichols reached for the letter and walked into the den with the handgun. He read the letter.

Dear Jim,

I owe friends and supporters a full accounting of my reasons for what I am about to do. I trust you know whom to show this letter to.

The coming trial threatens the continued existence of a valued organization and would lead to the premature deaths of scores of those who would otherwise be given the opportunity to live out their lives as God intended.

I cannot, in conscience, be the cause of those deaths. I have taken the path of death before. I have not told this to anyone in the Network before, but while still in medical school I attempted to perform an abortion on the fiancée of a close friend. They were in desperate straits. We agreed there was only one solution to the problem. I decided to attempt an abortion. But, afterwards, she hemorrhaged in her sleep and bled to death that night. The deaths of that child and mother eventually led me to the Resurrection Network. Death led me to dedicate myself to life.

Now one more death, mine, will save the lives of many and will allow the Resurrection Network to continue its mission. I prayed that this cup would pass me by. But God's will be done, not mine.

I undertake this action in a prayerful state. I realize that my course of action will be considered 'selfish' by some and 'heroic' by others. I trust and am confident in the knowledge that God approves of this course. This is not a worldly suicide to avoid the consequences of my actions. I am proud of what I have accomplished. I willingly embrace this sacrifice as a means of saving the lives of others more innocent than I.

But I want to sound a warning to all who believe as I do. Do not allow the righteousness of our cause have us adopt the tactics of our opposition. Let my death be the last death necessary to sustain the cause of the Resurrection Network.

Yours in Christ,
Dr. Frederick Nichols

Dr. Nichols signed and sealed the letter. Marked it *Confidential and Personal to the attention of James Fallon, Esq.* and left it on his desk. He then spent two hours organizing his legal and financial papers, including all his insurance policies and his will, placing them neatly on his desk. He spent several hours in prayer before reaching for the gun. He remembered Fallon's instructions and pointed the barrel before pulling the trigger.

The sound of the gun firing was louder than he imagined. Fallon reached for his phone and dialed 911 as he walked into the den and found Nichols on the floor.

McGuinness' EMT duty squad was thinly staffed that night. Early spring vacations and illness reduced the squad to two: the driver and McGuinness. They quickly responded to the call and pulled in front of Nichols house within minutes. In fact at the formal inquiry the hospital termed the quick response time as "dumb luck" because the unit was only blocks away refueling at a local gas station.

When the EMT unit arrived at the Nichols home, Luke McGuinness grabbed the emergency bag and quickly raced from the passenger seat to the house. He shouted to the driver to wait in the unit, not bring the stretcher, and leave the engine running. Once inside he met Fallon and Nichols.

"Hi Fred, are you OK?" McGuinness inquired of the bleeding Nichols.

Nichols' blood was trickling down his left arm. The bullet trajectory was aimed to pass through his arm causing no sustainable damage, just enough tearing causing him to bleed a lot and leave a huge stain on the area carpet. A flesh wound actually. Fallon had already started wrapping a bandage around the wound.

"Nice job on the wrap, Jim. You are a quick learner."

"Thanks, boss," Fallon responded.

Nichols smiled. "McGuinness, so good to see you… How did you get here so soon?" his voice trailed off as he looked at both men. "Jim what did you call McGuinness?"

"You got it, Fred," McGuinness interjected. "It's a quick story. I won the huge megabucks lottery a few years back. One ticket and one winner! And after a long time living it up and I mean really living it up, I came to my senses. Well, actually it was the auto accident that made me come to my senses. I was God's victim. It was a combination of two much alcohol, two beautiful blondes, a red hot Lamborghini and a steep curve outside of Arles, France. The blondes survived without a scratch. As for me, I was laid up for 9 months if you count the rehabilitation after the multiple surgeries. But it didn't take me long to realize that it was God's plan for me to survive that accident. You see, Fred, just like St. Ignatius of Loyola heard God's voice in a cave in Manresa, I heard God's voice in a countryside rehabilitation hospital in the south of France. He founded the Jesuits and I founded the Resurrection Network," McGuinness summed it up. "This is the result. We've done a lot these past years, saved and extended a lot of lives, and will continue to do so, thanks to your cooperation. By the way, I never saw the blondes again," he added with a smile.

"But the gun, the bullet, the note…"

"We want them to think you are a nutcase, deranged, and lost in your ethical acts. Makes your actions logical to a point. When you disappear, you will eventually be forgotten; talked about, but forgotten. Just like D.B. Cooper some 45 years ago…an urban legend. That's the only way to get the Network out of harm's way today." He took over the job of wrapping the arm and looking at Nichols said, "That does it. Let's get out of here."

Fallon promised to keep the police off guard as much as possible. Delay, obfuscate, and act bewildered: the hallmarks of a good executive. When all hell is breaking loose - Don't answer the question, look offended, and pled you have no idea what's going on.

McGuinness and a wobbly Nichols quickly walked to the van. It was a warm spring night. The sound of a police siren was in the distance. "They're on their way. We've got to move faster," McGuiness counseled. They quickly got into the back of the unit as the driver gunned the motor. They were around the corner and out of sight before the police arrived at the home. Fallon was inside waiting. Time to call on those acting classes he took at high school.

The patrolman blinked first. "We got a call about a gunshot and a wounded Dr. Nichols. Did you make the call?"

"Yes, for the record, my name is James Fallon. I'm an attorney and I represent Dr. Fred Nichols." He thought to himself that the longer he talked, the further away Nichols would get. He continued. "Although I'm a Connecticut resident, I also hold a Pennsylvania license to practice law…"

"What's going on? Who was shot? Where's the body?"

"Smart cops," Fallon told himself. "Why, didn't you pass the EMT vehicle?"

"What are you talking about, Mr. Attorney from

Connecticut?"

"The EMT unit already left. They're taking Dr. Nichols to the hospital. They went that way," he said pointing in the wrong direction. "I hope he'll be OK, but while you're here, take a moment to look around. Take inventory, secure the area. See, over there…blood samples and a bandage that was used to treat the body of my client, Dr. Nichols. Take liberty to check things out. The wound was devastating."

The police routinely searched the area. It was several more minutes before the desk officer at the station called. They informed him that Nichols had been shot and was probably at the hospital as they spoke and Nichols attorney was in the home at the time of the shooting. Following instructions, one police officer stayed behind while the other drove to the hospital. Twenty minutes had lapsed.

Meanwhile, the EMT unit pulled to the side of the road. A car was waiting for them. Nichols quickly exited the truck and entered the car. He was driven to a vacant private grassy area where a small Cessna aircraft was waiting for him. The plane was heading towards Altoona by the time the police arrived at the hospital. Altoona would be the first of five stops before he reached his final destination.

Later, in completing the hospital incident report, McGuinness stated that the EMT vehicle, while on the way to the hospital, swerved sharply to avoid hitting a deer that stood squarely in the middle of the right lane. The driver of the large vehicle tried to return the vehicle to the proper lane but due to the emergency speed of the vehicle and the wet pavement, the truck inadvertently slid off the road into the Lackawaxen River. Because the spring rain swelled the river to record highs that season, the van was partially submerged in the swift running water. McGuinness and the driver escaped the vehicle and were unhurt. However the rear door of the vehicle was sprung open and the gurney carrying Dr. Nichols was thrown from the unit. No one could locate Dr. Nichols's body. The gurney was located 50 yards downstream.

Later that morning Jim Fallon went to the Nichols home in a professional capacity. He located the letter on the desk in the den. He read it, chuckled quietly, and put it in his pocket. He left the house and waved it to the press who were gathered outside the house hoping for a sound bite or clue to help solve the bizarre happenings of several hours earlier.

****

Sidney Armstadt made a phone call to Steve Williams apprising him of the sad situation that had developed over Dr. Nichols disappearance. "A sorry state, Steve, a sorry state, for sure." He paused realizing he created alliteration with the letter "S". Momentarily he humored himself. "Our cause for drastic action has been somewhat derailed. Put on hold, if you will. A waiting game. Got to be careful to analyze the situation thoroughly, completely. Can't be irrational. Got to examine the facts before we spend any more time. Time is money. The facts, all of them," he said to a bewildered Williams.

"So what does that mean Sid? I mean how much money are we, am I going to make? After all, I am the father."

"Yes, a father you are, but, in this case, in this scenario, the obvious fact is that it is the mother who is grieving more than you. Totally defenseless, on her own, recovering from a drastic accident, a totally defenseless and innocent woman." He paused. "She gets first dibs on any money; she gets her hand on the pie before us, Steve. We're not looking too good, not good at all, in fact I'd say that all is lost, poof, gone, by a magician's hand, a blank stare into the darkness. No money."

"Are you saying that we're not going to get anything, Sidney?"

"Well Steve, you certainly look good in that sport coat and slacks I bought for you. You cut a mean figure, almost a crooner if you had a fedora, quite the looker. At no charge to you, either. My cost, my pocketbook, my loss. A deductible expense nonetheless. Kept the receipts for all of this. Wish you

214

the best young man. I'll keep track of this escapade and will call you if fortune points its fickle finger our way. If we get lucky. No doubt you'll hear from me."

Chapter 14

Dan Hewitt was being lowered to the ground on a hydraulic lift attached to the handicapped-accessible van that was hired to take him directly from the Lancaster Hospital to the Stoltzfus farm complex south of the city. Wallington had arrived about an hour earlier.

The van was parked on the property of the farmhouse, just a few feet from where, just two days ago, he had found the packing slip from Universal Pharmaceuticals.

Chief Wallington and several officers from the Lancaster County Sheriff's office along with local police were with Hewitt.

The area around the farmhouse was much changed since Hewitt's first visit. The high fence was gone; the playground equipment was non-existent and an area somewhat larger than that which the fence had enclosed had been scraped clean by construction equipment until it resembled the infield of a municipal baseball diamond. It was a natural farm yard. You couldn't tell where the fence posts had been or where the playground equipment had been installed. An Amish family was busy at work and play.

"What about the garage," asked Hewitt.

"I've been through it, Dan," said the chief. "It's a working garage...tools, some gas operated power equipment, the usual stuff you'd find and a lot of just plain garage junk."

Hewitt entered the garage through the dilapidated overhead door. Hewitt couldn't believe his eyes. The concrete floor was gone. The garage walls were unfinished, the sink, the freezer, the metal shelving, the drop ceiling—all gone. The air-conditioning vents, even the air-conditioning unit, had been removed. He was sitting in an old, decaying, working garage.

"I'm telling you, Chief, when I was here, this place was

some kind of storage room and lab and it had tons of medical supplies. I had the packing slip in my hand. This farm was some sort of medical clinic for children. There was playground equipment, ramps for wheelchairs. I can't believe what they've been able to do in so short a time. This is no small outfit we're dealing with. They've got bucks and manpower."

"You want to go into the house?"

"What'll I see?"

"Nothing. Looks like a house to me."

"Who owns the place?"

"The Stoltzful family has resided here for years. They farm, the acres behind the barn. Corn, Pennsylvania broad leaf tobacco...they have records showing sales to the John Hay Cigar Company down the road a ways. It's a big cigar maker, Dan."

"How can that be?"

"It is what it is, Dan."

"I want to inspect that barn."

"Let's go."

The contingent walked to the barn. Dan slid open the huge door.

"I fell through this unfinished..." He stopped in mid-sentence. The barn housed several horses, bales of hay. All on a finished but worn barn floor.

"There's a row of cows in the lower level along with an assortment of hay and feed and whatever," one of the deputies offered.

"I tell you, this is the place and this was not here two days ago." He thought for a moment. "Don't the Amish build a barn in two days or so? Could they have come here and re-built this farm complex?"

"Dan, anything is likely but that is not probable," the chief said as he scratched his head. "Would you care to speak with the owner, one Elias Stoltzfus?"

"No. These bastards are thorough. I'll give them that," said Hewitt. "Get me the hell out of here."

Four hours later, Hewitt had checked into Wayne Veterans Memorial Hospital and was resting in his room when Vivian Modell walked in.

"Hi, Dan, how are you feeling?"

"Better Viv. Surprised to see you, what with Dr. Nichols and all. I thought you and Fedderson would be busy all day."

"Actually, I'm just leaving his office. We've had a horrible day. The calls we've gotten. And the matter of the still missing Dr. Nichols.

"Did he leave a note?"

"Yes, more of a confession, a grim logical excuse for his involvement in the Network. His attorney was in the kitchen making a cup of coffee. He called the police immediately."

"Have you met this Fallon guy?"

"Yes, in fact Doug knows him."

"Does he?"

"Yeah, they know some of the same people. New York City types. They've bumped into each other before. Even have had some business dealings, apparently. Small world stuff."

"So what's he like?"

"Fallon? He's a big time player. Not slick or flashy just damn good. Comfortable in the limelight. Professional makes a point well, listens well, and he knows the law."

"How much time have you spent with him?"

"Is that a personal or professional question?"

"Oh, well professional," stammered Hewitt. "Never mind, sorry."

"I was just kidding with you. Don't get so flustered. Anyway, since Fallon arrived in town, let's see, that was the day of your accident..."

"Not an accident."

"Yes, I've heard you believe the hit-and-run driver deliberately ran you into that tree."

"Positive of it. Just not positive who did it."

"Whoever they are, I'm glad they failed. Anyway, I've spent an hour or two with Fallon, always with Fedderson."

"And you made all those judgments about him based on a couple of hours."

"Do you think cops are the only ones who have to take the measure of someone quickly?"

"No. As I remember you always did have good radar when it came to judging others."

"Not flawless, by any means. There was you."

"Oh, how far off the mark were you with me?"

"Pretty far. I thought you might be the one."

"The same thought occurred to me about you, Viv. That's when I started to let things go bad. You know, I've often thought that.... Well, never mind, that's all water under the bridge. You're with Fedderson now, and you seem happy."

"Well, I've got some news for you. You are sure to hear it from hospital staff anyway and I'd rather you'd heard it from me."

"Should I do a drum roll?"

"Doug and I are no longer an item."

"When did this happen?"

"I don't know. It's been a gradual thing over the past weeks. A lot of stress on both of us, the Franco thing, the missing baby, now a missing Dr. Nichols. The final break came the day you served Doug with the search warrant."

"So what happened? Never mind. I don't care what happened. Look Viv, I know that you must be upset about this, but I'd be lying if I told you I thought this was bad news. Fedderson was the only thing stopping me from seeing if we could start over."

"Oh, please, give me a little breathing room. I may be upset, a little anyway. Well, he and I are through. But let's not you and I rush into anything. Give me a little time. How long you going to be in that cast?"

"Eight, maybe 10 weeks, why?"

"I must say, I like the idea of having you in a position

where I can push you around. Well, I've got to go. Mind if I stop by tomorrow?"

"I was hoping you would. I should be discharged by one. After that I'll be at home."

"You got any help there?"

"No, I'm on my own."

"I'll give you a call. Maybe I can come by and we can rearrange the place so you can get around better."

"I'd like that, Viv," smiled Hewitt. "See you tomorrow."

"OK, tomorrow then. Bye."

****

Six weeks later Hewitt, as requested, rolled his wheelchair into Chief Wallington's office. He was surprised to see Henry Silva had arrived earlier.

"How's it going Dan?" said the prosecutor. "You're about due to get out of that cast, aren't you?"

"Two weeks. Can't wait," said Hewitt. "What's up, guys?"

"Dan, we wanted to discuss the amount of time you've been putting in on the Baby Franco case."

"I'm not going to like this, am I?"

"You've got to be reasonable, Dan. The computer search on Elias and Anna Stoltzfus has drawn a blank. We could find no record of a PA DMV registration: I JHN5-2. Just for the heck of it, even checked nearby New Jersey DMV. No luck there, either."

"But I did have a report showing that registration under the name of Stoltzfus living at that Lancaster farmhouse. I showed it to you, Chief, you saw it."

"Actually, Dan, you never really showed it to me. You held it up and told me about it. I discussed it with Henry. But if it comes to sworn testimony, I'd back you up, of course, I'd tell them you showed me the report. But the truth is, I never saw it. And my little white lie wouldn't do us much good anyway. We can't produce the original and the state police can't reproduce the same results. Besides the Elias Stoltzfus who lives at that farm is Amish. He doesn't drive a car. Gets around by horse and buggy. Better mileage than any red pick-up truck."

"Fine. What difference does that make? I can swear to the fact that I received the list from the State Police. They may have a record of the request."

"Yes, of the request, but not the response. You're the only one who saw the list. You're the only one who knows the Stoltzfus' were on it. We no longer have the list," said the Chief. "You know what a defense attorney could do with that type of representation in court."

"And you don't have the packing slip from Universal Pharmaceuticals, either," said Silva. "You said it was lost or mislaid at the scene of your car crash. Also, there were no fingerprints at the farmhouse or the garage. You've hit dead end after dead end."

"Look Dan, here's the thing," said the chief. "We can't afford to spend any more time on this one. We've got other active cases that need the work."

"You're closing the case."

"No, it remains open. Nichols' body hasn't been found. He could be washed up on the river bank somewhere downstream. The current was pretty strong that night. He could have survived the gunshot would, crept up on the river bank, stumbled around the forest and died under a log. The bloodhounds haven't found him and they had a good smell from the bloodied bandage wrap they found at his house. Somebody will find him sometime. This whole affair remains "Unsolved", but not a priority."

"They tried to kill me, Chief. It's a priority to me."

"I understand, I do. I know how you feel. But any work you do on this case from now on, it has to be on your own time. Or when things slow down. It's not being closed, just moved to a back burner for a while. Hey, you never can tell. Sometimes that's when a case breaks for you. You work on it day in and day out for months and then when you get away from it for a while, bingo. The solution jumps into your head."

"We've got the copy of the medical report Evans did on Baby Franco. That report shows the kid wasn't near death as Dr. Nichols claimed."

"That report has been misfiled and although Evans maintains the child was very ill, we have no factual report written at the time other than her recollection. And to complicate the matter even more, she may or may not have full recall because of possible memory fogginess, or whatever you call it because she had massive doses of anesthesia for surgery after her heart attack. No proof, Dan."

"I bet then that Fedderson is in on it, too. He's part of this. As the hospital administrator he may have diverted medical supplies from the hospital to that safe house."

"Dan we need evidence…"

"I'll get the evidence. But I can't do it if you shut me down."

"Damnit, Dan, every time you come to a blind spot in this investigation you throw in another conspirator. Be practical, you don't have enough to merit spending this amount of time or money on it."

"Chief, Henry, something is wrong here. They were waiting for me at that farmhouse. They knew I was on the way. How'd they know? Who told them? How'd they find out?"

"You don't know that for sure, Dan," said the chief. "It's just a hunch. You don't have any proof."

"My lack of proof proves the conspiracy," said Hewitt.

"Logic like that will get us far in court," said Silva.

"Henry, Chief, think about it. Look what they did to that house. How can you have a whole house with no fingerprints? What happened to the handicapped ramps, to the concrete floor in the garage, the drywall, the freezers, the air conditioning unit, the goddamn playground equipped with monkey bars and God knows, whatever else…and the eight-foot fence, the dumpster. Do you think I made all of that up? They cleaned that place out in a day. It's those Amish barnstormers and those barn tearing down clowns. I'm telling you there's money and plenty of manpower behind this crew."

"No, I don't think you made it up, but what the hell are we supposed to do? Keep spinning our wheels on this case while fresh leads on other crimes go stale? Get me something, anything solid. Universal Pharmaceutical has no record of any deliveries to anyone in southern Lancaster County, Pennsylvania."

"They nearly killed me to get the packing slip with all that information on it. I had it. I had the whole thing."

"'Had' don't cut it," said the chief. "What you've got is nothing. Even after you chased down every large order Universal Pharmaceutical has processed in the past five years you come up empty handed. None of those locations show any record of passing along an order to the farm house area."

"We've got large deliveries to Wayne Veterans Hospital where Dr. Nichols worked. Maybe he or Fedderson…"

"Again with Fedderson," said Silva throwing up his hands.

"Maybe Nichols, or Fedderson, or someone in the hospital, diverted shipments to that farm house and then destroyed the paper trail and altered computer records."

"Think of what would be involved in covering that up, Dan," said Silva. "Someone in procurement or finance would have to juggle the books. Drug orders are audited. Every capsule is accounted for, every cubic centimeter of prescription medicine."

"That's why I say Fedderson is in on it. It was very suspicious the way that heavy hitter lawyer showed up just when Nichols needed him. You know Fedderson and that lawyer knew each other. They even had some business dealings."

"Dammit, Dan," said the Chief, "you don't care who you drag into this investigation. A prominent out of town attorney with political connections...just what this case needs. Look, you can go on any wild goose chase you want to. Knock yourself out. But you do it on your own time."

"Think about what you have in terms of proof," urged Silva. "A pharmaceutical company with large shipments of drugs to a local hospital. That's all you can prove today. A defense attorney will be able to show hundreds of similar shipments to other hospitals. The hospital will be able to detail how those shipments were dispersed. Maybe you are right. This is a vast conspiracy and the conspirators covered their tracks. That's what criminals do. They destroy evidence, they leave false trails. Sometimes they screw up, maybe this time they didn't. I feel bad for you, Dan. I do. But that's the decision. No more time on this case, while you are assigned to any active case."

"Chief, I've got to ask you one question. I've got to ask it. Who else knew about my trip to the farm house? I told you and Prosecutor Silva. Did you tell anyone?"

"No," said the chief. "No one. You and I talked about it, you told Prosecutor Silva yourself while I was with you. Silva and I and discussed it before he went to see Judge Collins on the Dr. Nichols wiretap."

Prosecutor Silva stood up and walked to the window, leaned on the sill and looked out into the distance.

"Could anyone have overheard our conversation, Mr. Prosecutor?" asked Hewitt.

"Huh? I'm sorry. No. Quite impossible. No one else knew. You called me the evening before you went and early next morning, while you were on your way to Lancaster, I was with Judge Collins trying for the wiretap. There was no one I could have told."

"I don't know, maybe I'm going crazy" said Hewitt. "Maybe it was just a hit-and-run accident."

"I don't believe that, and I don't think you do either,"

said the chief.

"No, you're right, Chief, I don't. That guy caught my rear panel and just rode me into that tree," said Hewitt. "I'm telling you, the place was locked down tight, like they were expecting me. Maybe it's just my imagination."

"Well," said the chief, "unless you suspect Henry or me, or you mentioned the trip to anyone, there was no way they could have been notified."

Silva continued to look out the window.

****

"Prosecutor Silva to see you, Judge."

"Thank you, Diane, send him in."

A moment later Prosecutor Silva entered Judge Collins's chambers.

"Good to see you, Henry."

"I know what you did, Judge."

"Excuse me, Henry? Maybe you should close the door. Have a seat. Now, what's on your mind?"

"You got the number for the farmhouse in Lancaster, the one that Hewitt was going to. You called them. I don't know why you did, but you called. You didn't call from here. I've checked the billing records for the courthouse phones. I'm guessing you were too smart to phone from home either."

Judge Collins sat impassively.

"But I'll pull those records too, just in case. Either way, I know you called. You warned them, and they almost killed Hewitt. How far would you have let it go, Judge? What if Hewitt had died?"

"Whatever else you believe, Henry, you must know that I had nothing whatever to do with Hewitt's accident."

"You had everything to do with it if you called. Everything. And you had to know how dangerous they were after they took that child from the funeral home."

"You think the people who went after Hewitt are

225

involved in the missing children."

"Hewitt thinks so, no hard evidence of course, but he makes a persuasive argument."

"Sweet Jesus..."

"Why, Judge, can you tell me why? I know you, have known you for years. You wouldn't do this for money. What possible reason?"

"Forgive me, Henry, if I am not terribly forthcoming. What do you propose to do?"

"If your home phone records are clean..."

"I can assure you they are."

"Then there is nothing I can do. Oh, I could bring a case against you before a Grand Jury, but I don't think I have enough to get an indictment, let alone win at trial."

"You have enough to ruin my reputation and both our careers, Henry."

"You're right, Judge, if I bring charges against you, your career goes down the tubes followed closely by mine. I'm the one who gave you the information you used. I'm not into meaningless, ineffective, noble gestures. But tell me, Judge, what possessed you?"

"If I were to do such a thing," said the judge, "I suppose it would be for justice."

"You are an officer of the court, sworn to uphold the law. You can't serve justice by violating the law."

"Don't be silly, Henry. Sometimes the law gets separated from justice. When the two diverge, I try not to lose sight of justice completely."

"So that's it. You risk a police officer's life and you call it justice."

"Henry, we've known each other for more than 20 years. You know I would never knowingly do anything to harm a police officer or help a murderer."

"Ignorance is no defense."

"Well, Henry, we seem to be at an impasse. Do you have anything more for me today?"

"I just wanted you to understand you didn't get away with this. And I was hoping you could explain why, but that's too much to ask."

"Henry, I can't change the entire world. Neither can you. But what would you do if you could change one person's world for the better? I'm not talking about making life easier or offering a free ride. What if you could help someone who lost a chance to devote her life to something important? What if you could arrange for that person to do the difficult thing she desperately wishes she had done when she had the chance? Would you stretch the rules, take some chances?"

"It's Grace Bedford, isn't it?"

"If you could give someone a second chance at doing the right thing...would you?"

"Would I misuse my office...?"

"No, no, Henry. Use it in a most powerful, most beneficial way. Would you use your office to create good?"

"Whose good?"

"Mine, dammit. Is that what you want to hear, Henry? OK, then. My good. I am nearly 65-goddamn-years-old, Henry. Closing in on my threescore and ten. And I have the audacity to believe that I can recognize good. And I'll be damned if I'll apologize for it."

"Laws exist to protect the rest of us from personal concepts of good and evil that individuals would impose on us. Look at what you've done. You compromised an investigation and you nearly got Hewitt killed. "

"Unforeseen and unintentional, and I might add, unproven, Henry. Look, terrible things happen every day. Unspeakable horrors. Is it such a bad thing if once in a great while we are able to accomplish good despite the law?"

"Of course it's bad. It is up to society to deal with the injustices it creates."

"And if society does not recognize injustice?"

"All the more reason to fight injustice out in the

open. Not secretly, not by abuse of office or misuse of authority, but publicly. Stand up and challenge society to improve."

"I am surprised, Henry, with how much faith you put in the entire process. You know as well as I how imperfect this system is. You see its imperfections each day."

"I admit the system has flaws. But your methods undermine the entire structure, the elements that work as well as those that do not."

"Henry, I just don't have your faith or your patience."

"You know, Judge, if there were a way I could nail you on this I would."

"I don't doubt it for a moment, Henry. Not for a moment."

"One last thing, Judge," said Silva. "Pray Hewitt doesn't stumble onto the fact you made that call. If he does, we're both going down."

"Maybe you ought to offer him a job in the prosecutor's office. Keep an eye on him. He's a good man. Good day, Henry."

EPILOGUE

Joan Evans was enjoying lunch with Alan. Her recovery was almost complete and she would be returning to her practice on a part time basis within a week. The phone rang. It was Janice Franco, a jubilant Janice Franco, who exclaimed she was not only accepted into the LPN program but also received a full scholarship! Joan congratulated her and suggested they keep in touch. She was pleased that she wrote the recommendation for her admission and secretly funded the scholarship for her education. Of course no one except the school finance office knew of Joan's gift.

****

Luke McGuinness resigned his position at Wayne Veterans Hospital. In his letter of resignation, he cited his yen for travel at this critical time in his life. "If I don't go now, I never will," he wrote. He immediately re-settled to mid-America where he continues to finance the Network.

****

Philip Duran, James Fallon, and Doug Fedderson continue to serve the Network. Fedderson, however, accepted another position at a hospital somewhere in the south.

****

Dan Hewitt never solved the case. It remains on a back burner but occasionally he pokes around the various reports. Still baffled but he's moved on. He and Vivian have resumed their relationship.

****

Fred Nichols body was never found. No wonder. The flesh wound healed and he's a physician at a hospital in the northwest. Another name, same moral focus.

****

Joe Wallington never moved to his retirement home. He died of a massive heart attack five days before his retirement party.

****

Judge Collins stepped out of his car in an upper middle class neighborhood. Grace Bedford was in the front yard, tending to a small garden. There was a wheelchair ramp up the front steps of the modest Cape Cod home.

The judge paused at the gate. In the doorway of the home was a small child sitting in a wheelchair. There was an IV lead from a plastic bag hanging from a narrow post extending up from the rear of the chair. The child was motionless.

Grace turned at the sound of the judge's car door closing.

"Judge," she said brightly. "What brings you here today?"

"I decided to deliver the final adoption papers myself."

"Oh, my God, Judge. The final papers. How did you do this so quickly?"

"I'm a judge, Grace. I can do anything--except change the past."

"Emily," said a tearful Grace Bedford, holding up the adoption papers. "See? We're a family now. No one can take you away. Isn't that wonderful, Emily?"

At the sound of her name, Emily rocked gently back and forth in her wheelchair.

****

Baby Franco died two months later. She lived her life as peaceful as possible at a safe house about three miles outside of Honesdale. Before she died, she had been caressed and sung to by a smiling and grateful Joan Evans. Joan cried for an hour afterwards thanking God for the beauty of life.

THE END

Made in the USA
Middletown, DE
23 December 2016